Johanna Jones has lived in two houses in the Isle of Wight, Carisbrooke Castle and a labourer's cottage built in about 1800, so that the title of this book aptly fits her own experience. She has studied Island houses for thirty years, an interest that grew out of her lectures on Island social history for the Workers' Educational Association and the University of Southampton. Her research on on the Isle of Wight House of Industry led to an interest in cottage homes, whilst her study of farmhouses in the 1630 survey of Swainston Manor revealed much information about seventeenth century houses on the Island.

Johanna Jones's books about the Island are well-known. Together with her husband, Jack, she wrote what is generally regarded as the definitive history of the Island, *The Isle of Wight: An Illustrated History*. She contributed to *Farmhouses and Cottages of the Isle of Wight*, compiled by Marion Brinton, and has written an Island cookery book based on historical recipes.

FOLLOWING PAGES
A simple eighteenth century gentleman's cottage below St. Boniface Down, still retaining the feeling of the cottages and old farmhouses from which the genteel cottages derived. Thomas Bowdler, editor of *The Family Shakespeare*, lived here. His Shakespeare omitted everything that could not be read, 'with propriety', to the family.

CASTLES TO COTTAGES
The Story of Isle of Wight Houses

Johanna Jones

THE DOVECOTE PRESS

The Round House, Gurnard, was probably a toll house on the estate of George Ward, Northwood Park. Its rustic, fairytale appearance was designed to delight visitors as they approached the entrance to the park.

First published in 2000 by The Dovecote Press Ltd
Stanbridge, Wimborne, Dorset BH21 4JD

ISBN 1 874336 81 4

Text © Johanna Jones 2000

Designed and produced by The Dovecote Press Ltd
Printed and bound by the Baskerville Press, Salisbury

A CIP catalogue record of this book is
available from the British Library

1 3 5 7 9 8 6 4 2

Contents

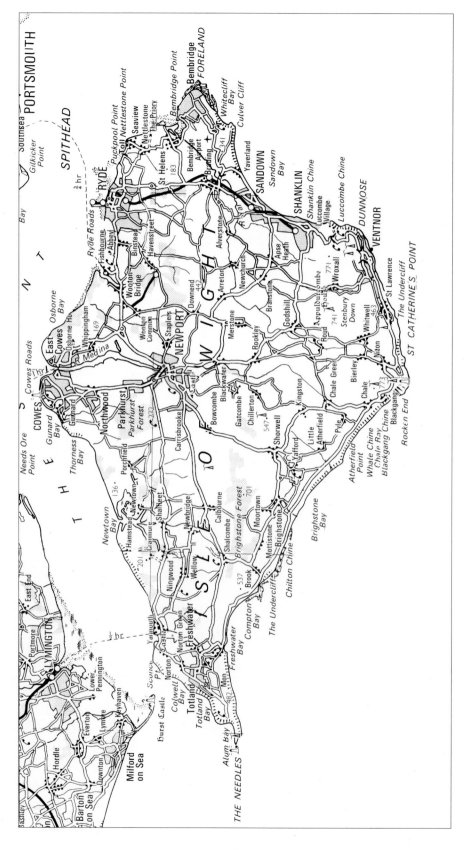

Shadows and Fragments of Early Houses

When our earliest ancestors first put a roof over their heads they began that long progress in domestic comfort which has led to the many conveniences we enjoy today. A timber hut with a thatched roof and neighbours nearby gave stability to prehistoric people. Farming and trade developed, the population increased, and the community created forms of government to protect and advance their embryonic societies.

Only archaeology can suggest how the earliest communities lived: of their homes almost nothing remains. Neolithic farmers had established themselves in the Isle of Wight by the third millennium BC but only their burial mounds and fragments of pottery give a hint of their lives and deaths.

Rather more can be deduced from archaeological evidence found unexpectedly on Gore Down when a new road from Niton to Chale was being laid in 1932. Workmen cut through a section of a late Bronze Age round hut, revealing the large post hole which had carried the central support to the roof. Traces of other huts and fragments of pottery indicate that in about 1000 BC there was extensive settlement in this southern part of the Island. The remains of much later Celtic settlement is equally sparse, with only the hillfort on Chillerton Down and a site at Knighton to remind us of the communities who lived here in about 100 BC. But less than one hundred and fifty years later the Island Celts were to experience for the first time a sophisticated and highly organized way of life when the Island was absorbed into the Roman Empire by Vespasian, the general who conquered much of southern England. And with the Romans came stone buildings, some of which have survived, to give us our first reliable evidence of a family home.

Where the majority of Roman villas, or farms, were built tells us much about the farming history of the Island. Of the surviving known villas five lie on the southern side of the central downs from Brighstone to Newport; the villa at Brading is also set at the base of the downs facing south. Only Combley was found on the north side of the downs but this, as its name indicates, was sheltered in its valley. All were self-sufficient farms drawing their livings from the rich greensands, which generations of later farmers would value in the same way.

Excavations have shown the types of houses in which these Romano-British farmers lived. At Rock above Brighstone there was a two storey stone building. Newport villa had a half-timbered wing, as did Brading in a long detached building. Even broken fragments of household ware can indicate the standard of living in houses which have disappeared. A tiny fragment of glass found at Bowcombe represented the head of a hound and was shown to be part of a fine glass bowl decorated with a classical scene depicting Actaeon being hunted by hounds. This was a valuable imported piece made in Alexandria and reflects a comfortable standard of living. More

8

ABOVE The bathrooms in Newport villa were reconstructed from building material found on the site. On the left was the cold plunge bath which bathers took before they entered the next warm room. From here they went directly to the hottest room, on the right, near the furnace. From here they returned to the next door room where sweat and dirt were scraped away and the skin soothed with sweet oils. A final cold plunge and bathing was complete.

OPPOSITE PAGE This decorative Roman mosaic floor was discovered in the grounds of Carisbrooke vicarage and excavated in 1859. It probably dates to the fourth century AD and is a fine example of mosaic work, with tiny tesserae creating the patterns. Sadly, exposure and neglect have destroyed a greater part of the floor, which can no longer be seen by the public.

obviously, the remains of mosaic floors and painted walls show us how attractive the interiors of these houses could be. The aisled villa found in the garden of Carisbrooke Vicarage in 1859 included an elaborate and beautiful floor with panels of flower buds and leaves surrounding a central vase. The more famous and intriguing floors at Brading villa were laid in a splendid, many-roomed corridor house, one side of a large courtyard with buildings on three sides. This is the largest Island villa, although Combley, too, had a large courtyard; but the villa which gives the most

revealing and intimate view of Romano-British farmhouse life lies, incongruously, surrounded by twentieth century suburban villas on the outskirts of Newport. It is the small size of this house which evokes a response from the visitor; the arrangement of rooms and the plain decoration speak of ordinary people leading ordinary lives.

The corridor house with two wings was built of stone with a box-framed upper level filled with wattle and finally lime-washed. One wing was given to the bath block, where three heated rooms had hot air circulating below the floors and around the walls. The amount of space devoted to bathing indicates more than an obsession with cleanliness, here one could relax, enjoy conversation, shut out damp and cold in the worst months of the year and emerge refreshed to rejoin the family.

Keeping warm meant that villas in Britain had to adapt to the climate. It is not surprising to find the living room in the main corridor wing placed against the walls of the bath rooms to share heat from the hypocaust system. Later the family added a fireplace with a hood and a hearth, which, if not very efficient as there was no real chimney, gave an illusion of extra comfort. A tessellated floor filled a central space, whose small pieces of chalk and

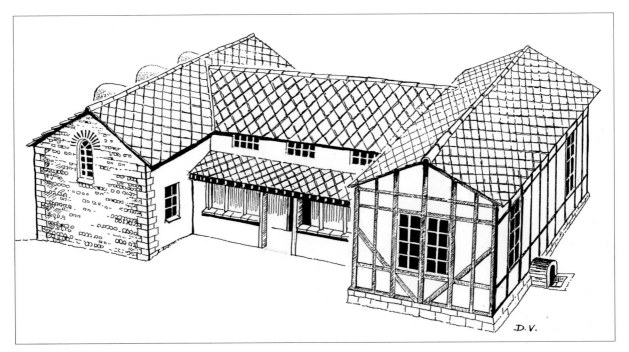

ABOVE A reconstruction of Newport Roman villa in Cypress Road. It was excavated in 1926-27 under the direction of Percy Stone, architect and antiquarian. A public appeal to preserve the villa was made, and this, together with generous help from Mr J.C. Millgate who covered the excavations, allows us to see today an attractive Romano-British farmhouse.

BELOW A thirteenth century window seat in the north wall of Carisbrooke Castle. This was part of the new 'high chamber' made for Countess Isabella between 1272 and 1276. Leaded panes of glass filled the window which looked down on Carisbrooke.

chopped red tile, were laid in a checker pattern, creating the effect of an inlaid carpet. There were also indications of painted panels decorating the wall.

This farmhouse seems to have had a life span from the second century AD until its final decay in the fourth century, together with the other Island villas. The collapse of the Roman Empire left its extreme borders vulnerable to attacks by invaders, in the case of the Isle of Wight first from the Jutes and later the West Saxons. Both these societies built in wood and no evidence of their domestic buildings remains apart from the postholes of a Saxon hall which once stood in what is now the courtyard of Carisbrooke Castle.

Wooden buildings were to provide homes for most people from Saxon times to the late eighteenth century but evidence of simple

The hall in Carisbrooke Castle as it might have been in the thirteenth century. A twelfth century window seat looks out onto the Keep and can still be seen today, and part of the stairs to the Great Chamber also remain. Behind the curtained archway was the chapel of St Peter, built by Isabella de Fortibus, Lord of the Isle of Wight from 1262-1293.

domestic buildings in the Island is rare. Early medieval houses in towns and villages were not built to last, many were so slight that they could be moved from place to place with ease. We have one example of just such a removal in 1250 when a house in Newport was set on rollers and dragged to a new site in the town. It was only royalty, the nobility and princes of the church who could build to last and some fragments of their early stone castles and manors do remain. In Carisbrooke Castle a twelfth century two light window at the dais end of the hall provided a window seat looking out to the Keep; and at Swainston Manor, Calbourne another two light window can still be seen in a building once used by the twelfth

century bishops of Winchester.

Carisbrooke Castle has a second stone window seat made in the thirteenth century for Countess Isabella de Fortibus, the remarkable woman who was Lord of the Island from 1262-1293. During her lifetime she made many improvements to domestic life in the castle, putting a well house over the well in the courtyard, building a new kitchen with a louvre in the roof, an embryonic chimney with slits or holes, a great improvement on kitchens where smoke had to escape through the eaves' space. The elegant window seat revealed in the Victorian restoration of the castle lighted her new 'high chamber' built against the north wall of the castle between 1272-76. The accounts detailing the work show that this window was filled with leaded panes of glass, a new luxury only enjoyed by the greatest of the nobility. Change in medieval society is illustrated by the position of the countess's new chamber, sited some distance from the hall. Gradually noble families were detaching themselves from the

general life of the household centred on the great hall. This did not mean that the position of the hall was diminished. It remained the formal reception room in the castle and its importance in the later Middle Ages is shown in the large finely carved stone fireplace built at the end of the fourteenth century by William de Montacute, Earl of Salisbury, then Lord of the Isle of Wight.

Outside the walls of the Castle there are only a handful of domestic buildings remaining from the medieval period. At Swainston an upper floor hall was built in the late thirteenth century, and a large three light window can still be seen in the north gable. In the garden of Wolverton, St Lawrence, there are remains of a small upper floor hall dating to the early fourteenth century with a traceried window in the north gable wall. Chale Abbey farm, the site of the manor house built by John de Langford, Constable of Carisbrooke Castle in the early fourteenth century, also has a window in the north gable wall. Like Wolverton it had an undercroft and an annexe at an angle to the main building. We are fortunate that any fragments of these early buildings can be seen today. They survive because they were strongly

built but, more importantly, because they were of practical value to later owners. Buildings that were not useful simply disappeared.

Some buildings, even of wood, that belong to the late Middle Ages and the beginning of the Tudor period do still remain – even if sometimes concealed within later building. Haseley Manor has a fine medieval wood frame building safely contained within later additions to the house. In Brading we can see from the main street an example of extravagant use of timber at the end of the Middle Ages. Part of the Wax Museum shows us the house of Jermyn Richards, a rich merchant, built in about 1500. His ostentatious use of wood was structurally unnecessary but it showed his neighbours that he was a man of substance. So too did his use of brick instead of common wattle and daub as infilling for the studding. Brick was still an unusual building material in 1500, employed only by wealthy men who were building or re-building castles and manor houses. The birth of brick as a major building material began at about the time Jermyn Richards was building his house.

What few visible remains there are of medieval dwellings tell us little about the life

OPPOSITE PAGE The late fourteenth century fireplace in the hall at Carisbrooke Castle was built for William de Montacute, Earl of Salisbury.

RIGHT A late medieval house at Brading. The building on the left with its gable facing the road is an example of extravagant building in wood. The upper floor was jettied over the ground floor and gave more space to the hall where the family lived. Later buildings were added and it now forms part of the Wax Museum, Brading.

that was lived within them and virtually nothing about the homes of ordinary people. Two fragments of life in the fourteenth century have been rescued for us by Dom Frederick Hockey, the historian of Quarr Abbey; one of a manor house family and one of a farming family. In 1349 John de Insula of Gatcombe died and from his will his widow Joan learned what parts of the manor house were to be hers during her widowhood. She was to have a chamber at the western end of the hall, and a small chamber at the eastern end which had an upper room and a fire place, the one which was known as the 'Norycerie'. Joan had a six year old son and the luxury of a heated room must have added much comfort to them both.

The farmer John Hardynge and his wife Joan moved to a farm at Rowborough just north of Shorwell in 1400. Together with Richard Paslowe they took the holding on a lease for three lives, which ceased when the last of three persons named in the lease died. Rowborough was part of the extensive landholdings of Quarr Abbey and the Hardynges appear to have been the first leaseholders of this grange. The house and barn were in a poor state and as part of their agreement they undertook to restore them both, while Quarr took no rent for the first year. Thereafter they paid £1.75 to Quarr, 50p to the prior of Carisbrooke and 1lb of cumin to the Abbess of Lacock, all of which related to the time in the late thirteenth when the grange was created.

Instructions for building the house and barn were set out by Quarr. The main building was to be four bays long, a bay being a variable measurement, but often about 16ft long. In the centre was a small hall for living and there was to be a small chamber on the upper floor. On the ground floor they had space for eight oxen and four horses and, as the oxen alone required as much as two bays, space for the family was rather less than that allotted to the animals. All were under one roof, the family rooms probably separated by a wide passage running from the front to the back of the house.

The written description of the steading on the slopes of Rowborough Down is more valuable to us than visible remains of the middle ages. It describes a working farmhouse whose plan already had a long history before 1400. The practicality of combining family and beasts under one roof ensured that it continued in some form for the next two centuries and it makes a convenient link between the homes of peasant farmers in medieval times and the farmhouses of their descendants, the Elizabethan and Jacobean yeomen farmers.

TWO

The Yeoman Farmer's House

What was a yeoman farmer? The medieval origins of a yeoman refer to an important servant or someone who served in the guard of a noble or royal person, hence the Yeomen of the Guard who attend the Queen. The use of yeoman to describe a particular type of countryman gradually evolved during medieval times until by the fifteenth century he was a distinct part of the social hierarchy below knights and squires, a freeholder working a small landholding. Gradually this definition was blurred until yeoman came to define any worthy countryman who cultivated his land well and lived comfortably. This best describes the yeomen farmers of the Isle of Wight during the sixteenth and seventeenth centuries. Few of them were freeholders, but tenancies for three lives and new tenancies lasting as long as eighty years gave enterprising men opportunities to improve both their farms and their homes.

The process had begun when farmers such as the Hardynges at Rowborough exchanged work on the manor as rent to money rent, which meant they could devote all their time to their own holding. Gradually shrewd farmers amalgamated their strips in the open fields into convenient single blocks which could be enclosed and worked separately from their neighbours. The Isle of Wight was being enclosed by the early years of the sixteenth century. In 1545 the land was described, probably with some exaggeration, as being 'full of edgerows', but around St Helens there were genuine complaints of land being enclosed within the common fields. By the early seventeenth century land was being enclosed on the lower slopes of the downs. On the northern clay lands where woodland was common isolated farmhouses surrounded by enclosed fields had by this time a long history.

Farmhouses and farm buildings were still built in wood. Their construction demanded

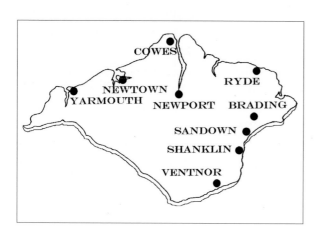

ISLE OF WIGHT TOWNS. The medieval towns were Brading – the first to be founded, by William Fitz Stur and before 1150; Newport, founded by Richard de Redvers, 2nd Earl of Devon, in about 1160; Yarmouth, also founded by de Redvers but slightly before Newport; and Newtown, founded by Aylmer de Valence, Bishop of Winchester, probably in 1255. The other towns are Cowes, which began life in the early seventeenth century; Ryde, which grew rapidly in the Regency period; Ventnor, which began life in the 1840s but had to wait for the coming of the railway in 1866 before it could develop; and Sandown and Shanklin, which did not exist as seaside towns until the arrival of the railway in 1879.

large numbers of trees, mostly young growth with the required measurements for structural and internal use. Some indication of the effect of an ever increasing demand for timber could be found in Brighstone in 1630. Tenants on the Swainston estate had not one piece of woodland recorded when the estate was surveyed in that year. The surveyor, John Harrison, was so concerned that he left instructions that, 'the steward . . . enquire what young trees are planted at Brixton; and encourage them to plant every year.'

Some parts of these wooden structures still remain. Valleys Cottage, Whitcombe, can be dated to the early seventeenth century when John Valleys became its tenant. Arreton Cottage, which lies on the main Sandown road, looks like a neat Victorian house, but the back wall is part of the original wood-framed building, once filled with wattle and daub, set on its solid stone sill. The house was cased in brick in the eighteenth century, leaving only the unimportant back wall untouched.

Arreton Cottage, Arreton. This Victorian-looking cottage conceals a history which dates to the seventeenth century. Behind the later brick walls the whole house is wood-framed.

The drawing below of the rear wall shows the original box-frame on a stone sill.

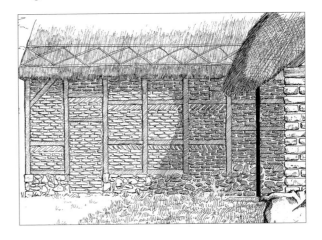

An earlier farmhouse can be seen at Elmsworth, Porchfield. This house was already old when it was surveyed by John Harrison in 1630. Its description, 'a hall with a chimney and two little rooms, and two rooms over' fits

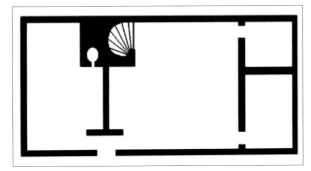

ABOVE Plan of a typical seventeenth century Island farmhouse. The entrance faces the central chimney stack. The kitchen fireplace includes a bread oven. The milkhouse and buttery are on the right.

OPPOSITE PAGE TOP Guyers, Shalfleet, as it was in the 1940s. The name is a legacy of Margaret Guyer, the tenant in 1630 when it was a farmhouse. The oldest part is on the extreme right.

OPPOSITE PAGE BOTTOM Dyrtshot, Atherfield. The chimney placed slightly to one side of the entrance door indicates that it backs onto one wall of a through-passage leading to the back of the house. This farmhouse is included in the 1630 survey of Swainstone manor.

BELOW Mill Farm, Bembridge, follows the seventeenth century farmhouse plan, with a central chimney stack in line with the entrance, and the stairs between the wall and chimney stack. The upper windows are Victorian, as is the porch.

the portion of wood framing which may still be seen today, though now part of a much larger house. It is a reminder of how small an early Tudor farmhouse could be, even one such as Elmsworth with a large and valuable acreage of woodland attached.

The seventeenth century yeoman farmer's house might be an old house in which the hall was still the only room with a fireplace, and therefore both kitchen and living room. Other families continued to cook in the medieval detached kitchen, sometimes under the same roof as the stable or barn. But a new house plan was supplanting these older buildings. The seventeenth century farmhouse was a compact dwelling with a hall, one or two chambers, with rooms overhead, and often with its kitchen within the main house. The most distinctive feature of these houses, one easily recognized today, was the central chimney stack emerging from the roof of a simple rectangular building. This functional and comfortable house evolved from the open plan of the medieval manor house. The central open hearth was abandoned by the later middle ages and a new fireplace with a chimney was set at the lower end of the hall backing onto the

Shate Place, Brighstone, a modern house in 1630. The original entrance was in line with the chimney. This was the home of Joan Baker, the Brighstone miller, a rich woman who could afford a house with a hall, parlour and an internal kitchen – all with fireplaces. Upstairs were five chambers, one with a fireplace.

service passage which led from the entrance to the back of the building. By the end of the sixteenth century in many farmhouses this passage disappeared, the space being used to build back to back fireplaces which could heat the hall and one other room, usually the new internal kitchen.

A few of the older houses which continued to separate the hall and chamber with a through passage from the front to the back of the house remain today. Street Place, well off the road near Calbourne, has a flattened Tudor arch over one exit door in its passage, whilst at Dyrtshot, Atherfield, another through passage house may be seen. Berrycroft Farm, Roud, near Godshill, has the parlour separated by a wide passage from a lower set of working rooms.

But the typical late sixteenth and seventeenth century farmhouse opened into a small lobby formed by the wall of the central chimney stack immediately opposite the door. The chimney emerged through the roof directly in line with the front door, unlike the through passage house where the chimney was set slightly to one side. A great deal of internal space was taken up by the large fireplaces which backed onto each other and by the solid chimney stack as it rose through the upper rooms. In the small space between the fireplace and the back wall of the house narrow stairs led upstairs. Few Island farmers could afford more than two fireplaces and evidence from the Swainston survey shows that most chose to use the second one for their kitchen, removing forever the need to cook in the hall or to carry food from the external kitchen of earlier times. Where money was plentiful more fireplaces were built. One of the grandest houses was Shate Place,

Brighstone, where Joan Baker, the miller, had a house with a heated hall, parlour and kitchen and one chamber upstairs with a fireplace.

Another example of a prosperous farmhouse is Fullingmills Farm, Calbourne. This house included a new parlour wing, 'all fairly built of stone', with a cellar, a parlour with a fireplace, a chamber above with a fireplace and a garret over this. This most advanced addition to the older house was as bold a statement of well-being as one could make and reflects the good husbandry of its builder. It was the home of John Jeeve, who leased half the Swainston demesne lands and was busy setting up new holdings to increase his income. But the typical Island yeoman's house consisted of a hall with one other room for the family at one end and at the other end of the hall one or two unheated service rooms commonly called a buttery and milkhouse. Above stairs were the unheated chambers which led directly into each other.

Many of these farmhouses remained completely unaltered well into the twentieth century. Externally they remain as they were built, with long low windows protected from the rain by their flattened dripstones. The thatched roofs have gone but the stone kneelers which supported the thatch can often be seen. The ground floor plan is likely to be unchanged and it is only upstairs that the insertion of a

Fullingmills Farm, Calbourne. This gable wing was added to an older house in the early seventeenth century. It gave the family a parlour, a chamber over it with a fireplace and attics. The relieving arches over the windows drew the pressure of the roof onto the walls and ensured that the windows retained their horizontal lines.

The quartered ceiling in the parlour at Fullingmills. The moulded beams show the high quality of this wing. John Jeeve, the tenant of Fullingmills in 1630, built the parlour wing. It celebrated a lifetime of successful farming in which he established two new farmsteads.

passage cut from the old rooms has met modern demands for privacy. The most common interior features that remain are the virtually immovable objects, the fireplace and the beams. Many open fireplaces were gradually filled in, until the recent enthusiasm for restoration brought them to light again.

A seventeenth century fireplace in New Inn, Shalfleet. A large bread oven was inserted later.

The fireplace took up much of the wall space and was the focus of life in a room. Well dressed stone jambs supported a flattened arch lintel or a massive wood beam above the flat hearth, where iron andirons carried the large logs. The back wall was protected from the direct heat of the fire by an iron fireback. In more affluent houses where the fireplace was new masons cut and moulded the jambs and included simple linear cut decoration in the lintel. But the most living link with the past is found in simpler hearths where one stone block can sometimes be seen partly worn into a concave curve by generations of men who sharpened their tools in comfort while they sat by the fire.

Just as fireplaces represented progress in domestic comfort the beams of a yeoman's

house tell us something of the building's age and of its owner's social standing. The young oaks were chosen with care before they were felled so that they met the required size and needed as little cutting as possible. The bark was stripped and the wood dressed to the right size. No sharp angles appeared on the exposed part of the beam, it was cut back, or chamfered, for the whole length and it is this work which gives a general indication of the age of a beam. Deep chamfers up to three and a half inches are found on beams made in the early years of the seventeenth century, later beams have narrower chamfers. End finishings called stops were made at the point where the beam enters the wall. Most stops were simple, often shield shaped, but there was scope for the carpenter to display decorative cutting, including a pretty heart stop which can still be found in some houses today. Exceptionally wealthy farmers such as John Jeeve at

Style House, Arreton. This large farmhouse stands near Arreton Church and close to Arreton Manor. Although the windows are modern they occupy the spaces of the original windows. The porch is eighteenth century but the entrance door is seventeenth century.

The photograph below shows the unaltered original windows in the back wall of the house.

Fullingmills had more decorative beams. His new parlour ceiling was quartered and all four beams which met in the centre were finely cut and moulded.

Even now we still find it easy to relate to these seventeenth century houses. They are real family homes built to a scale and plan that we feel comfortable with today. Our interest is enhanced because for the first time in domestic history we know in some detail how they were furnished and how the families lived. Many inventories of household goods list the main items in each room, allowing us an insight into how the rooms were used. In all cases the hall was the most important room. By this time the old table on trestles had been replaced by a 'tableborde with a frame', a permanent piece of furniture with legs and stretchers. With this were stools and benches for the household and only two chairs for the master and mistress. Some farmhouses such as Hill Farm, Brading, had 'stained' [painted] cloths hanging on the walls; Luccombe Farm included a carpet to cover the table and here, as at Marsh Place, Brighstone, the wooden seats were eased by cushions. The hall was the place of the musket and powder flask, the halberd, a combined spear and axe, and body armour such as helmets. It was also where the Bible, prayer book and psalter were kept for daily use. Farming families could by this time afford many pieces of pewter and brass and the love of flowers appears in entries such as two 'flower pottes of pewter'.

Although the word parlour occasionally appears it is clear that it differed little from a chamber, both of which were combined sleeping and storage rooms. At Style House, Arreton, the ground floor chamber included two four poster beds, one with a truckle bed kept underneath it when not in use. There were three storage chests for linen and clothes and a variety of household items; a still, a pair of large scales, tubs, sieves of various kinds and two saddles. Even a well-to-do farmer such as John Rawlings who lived there in 1607 could not afford to have a room just for sleeping. Kitchens were often well equipped. They included cauldrons, brass pans and pots, longhandled skillets for simmering in hot ashes, dripping pans to catch the juices from the food on the spit and the indispensable 'mortar and pestle' to hammer everything from meat to herbs into an edible form.

These self-sufficient farming households were dependent on a type of mixed farming based on downland sheep runs, grain on the greensands, dairy farming on the northern clays, with some sheep near the coastal grazing land. Wheat, barley, oats and beans, cattle, horses. pigs, geese, ducks and chickens could all be found in the fields and farmyard and the life of the household was bound to the seasonal work. It was a pattern of country living which was virtually unaltered until the middle of the nineteenth century. This long continuity of daily life meant that there was little need to change a house which functioned well.

THREE

Plain and Pleasing – Eighteenth Century Houses

Between 1700 and 1800 Britain changed dramatically. The big open fields of medieval times were gradually constrained into compact hedged fields. Great estates reshaped their parks, opening up vistas of carefully planted woods, new lakes and serpentine water courses. In the towns the change was equally visible: wooden houses disappeared, sometimes destroyed by fire, but more often hidden behind new brick facades. Streets were laid out in terraces lined with houses that were very different from their medieval predecessors. Much of this change was the result of government policy following the Fire of London.

In 1667 the Act regulating the rebuilding of the city imposed standards of fireproofing which changed the external appearance and internal plan of London town houses. Brick, a good fireproof material, replaced stone and wood and the height of storeys was defined. In the early eighteenth century the thickness and height of party walls was also fixed, wooden eaves were forbidden and the roof was hidden behind a parapet wall, while wooden windows and door frames were set back at least four inches from the outside face of the wall. In the wake of these regulations the new street frontage of London gradually evolved, and where the capital led the remainder of the country gradually followed.

Two external features immediately distinguish these houses from older buildings; the altered roof shape and the position of the chimneys. Gable ends were replaced with hipped roofs, wide and deep, which allowed dormer windows to light the attics. Elsewhere in the house tall sash windows replaced horizontal casements. The central chimney stack was abandoned and chimneys moved to the outer ends of roofs. This left space in the centre of the house for a staircase and allowed a balanced arrangement of rooms on the ground and upper floors.

These elegant new houses reflected the social status of those who lived in them. Elizabethan and Jacobean manor houses and farmhouses may have differed in scale, but they shared the same materials, the same shape of doorways and windows and much the same internal plan. They represented cohesion in a society which had its origins in the medieval past and only began to disintegrate at the time of the Civil War. The eighteenth century ended that sense of community as opportunities to make money from government appointments, trade, industry and agriculture, began the process of dividing society into distinct social categories.

All these factors can be found in the Isle of Wight. The old stone manor houses remained, now surrounded by hedged fields and many now beginning their decline into mere farmhouses. Others disappeared to be replaced by more modern buildings.

Gatcombe House, built in the 1750s by Sir Edward Worsley, is an example of the square 'blockish' mansion house fashionable in the second half of the century. It is a plain building with many carefully placed windows, rusticated quoins, a hidden roof line and a

Gatcombe House in 1823. This Georgian house was built in the 1750s by Sir Edward Worsley, a junior member of the Appuldurcombe family. A Venetian window breaks the formal line of windows and was recorded in place at the end of the nineteenth century by Percy Stone. It has since been replaced by conventional sashes and can now be found at the back of the house lighting the staircase well.

triangular pediment over the entrance to complete the classical design. Old Osborne House, Queen Victoria's and Prince Albert's first Island home was similar, but generally the Island gentry preferred their new houses to have evolved from the domestic style of later seventeenth century architects.

Thorley Manor, near Yarmouth was one such house. It was built in 1712 by Henry Holmes, nephew of Sir Robert Holmes, Governor of the Island. Following his uncle's death Henry married Sir Robert's daughter Mary and inherited the Thorley estate. With its hipped roof and upstanding chimney stacks, it reflects

the charm of an architectural style first introduced into England by Inigo Jones in the reign of James I. This western corner of the Island has a cluster of similarly fine houses as, apart from Thorley Manor, Henry Holmes rebuilt an older house next to Yarmouth Castle, now the George Hotel, and in Freshwater parish Afton Manor and King's Manor are both attractive examples of this style.

At the other end of the Island Sir William Oglander was bringing Nunwell up-to-date. The entrance front was transformed into a handsome facade with a deeply rusticated Baroque doorway. The roofline was raised to accommodate tall sash windows and the frontage brought up to date with red brick. However, behind the greater part of this wall the old Tudor wall remained, faced in a layer of mathematical tiles. Such tiles were a new feature, and although no cheaper than brick they were ideal for covering older parts of

ABOVE Thorley Manor, Yarmouth, is distinguished by four tall chimneys rising from the hipped roof with its deep eaves. These features, together with the tall windows and the round windows either side of the door, were used in superior domestic buildings from the second half of the seventeenth century.

BELOW Nunwell House. The entrance front with its sash windows, classical doorway and red bricks was created in the eighteenth century. The bricks are, in fact, mathematical tiles, hung on an older wall, transforming it into a fashionable frontage.

buildings. This new skin of tiles, no more than half an inch thick, was in the style of Flemish Bond, with alternate headers and stretchers, and is so convincing that it was only revealed when electricity cables were laid through Nunwell's walls.

Where there was height and space dramatic alteration was possible. At North Court, Shorwell, the large seventeenth century house was unaltered externally but eighteenth century visitors were received in a new hall designed in the classical style, with a high ceiling, flagged floor and curved archways leading to the staircase wing and rooms at the back of the house.

Although farming was improving at the beginning of the eighteenth century few Island farmers could afford to build in the grand new style. There is one exception, however, that of Great Park, Carisbrooke. The old medieval deer park was not sold until 1651 and it was only in the early years of the next century that a new house was built. It did retain part of an earlier house, the hall, which became the farmhouse kitchen, but this was hidden behind the new frontage with its deeply hipped roof, tall chimneys and balanced sash windows. In this new wing Great Park was given a drawing room and dining room on each side of an entrance hall which carried a wide staircase to the upper floors.

Not all new frontages could achieve this symmetry. At Horringford, just south of Arreton, the arrival of new owners, William and Mary Cromwell, saw work begin on a drawing room, entrance hall and one other room in the front of the house. Their initials and the date 1708 in the date stone over the

Great Park, Carisbrooke. This typical early eighteenth century house stands alone in its fields. It replaced an earlier house, part of which now forms the farm kitchen. Great Park was still a deer park when it was sold in 1651 and in the early years of the next century it became a farm.

A view of Horringford, Arreton, showing the eighteenth century addition to the older house. The right-hand gable end and the central chimney were part of the seventeenth century house. The lower windows light the kitchen, once the hall, looking onto the farmyard. The hipped roof on the left replaced part of the old house, giving Horringford a fashionable frontage in 1708.

front door commemorate their work. There were problems linking the new front with the old hall at the back of the house, which now became the kitchen overlooking the farmyard. The new entrance hall had to connect with an older passage to the kitchen and the old spiral staircase which crept round the chimney stack. This governed the position of the new entrance hall and front door and explains why Horringford has an unbalanced eighteenth century front.

Limerstone Farm, between Brighstone and Mottistone, has a fined hipped roof similar to Horringford, but here the whole aspect of the house was changed to look westward. The low Tudor casement windows remained. Farmhouses built in the sixteenth and seventeenth century were unable to change the height of windows without drastically reconstructing the interiors. Their low ceilings made vertical sliding sashes difficult to insert, so they retained horizontal casements which, by the end of the eighteenth century had developed a distinctive style: a shallow arch, usually wood in the Island, set above wood-framed windows.

In the countryside new houses began to appear which reflected the rising status of the Anglican clergy. At the end of the seventeenth century more than half the parish livings in England were worth less than eighty pounds a year and the parson lived much as a farmer, cultivating his glebe land and receiving his annual tithe. But in the eighteenth century the gentry and aristocracy began filling vacant livings with their sons and other relations. The attraction of a career in the church was as much economic as religious. The value of land

Gatcombe Rectory. In 1708 John Worsley became rector of Gatcombe and the old parsonage house was altered to suit his social standing. A drawing room, dining room and entrance hall were built with a fashionable frontage, whilst the old hall became the kitchen.

was rising, good harvests in the early part of the century and an increasing demand for wool enhanced farm profits and the local parson shared in this prosperity through his tithe income. Meanwhile, old clergy houses had either disappeared or were unsuitable for the new incumbents.

Gatcombe parish in the early eighteenth century exactly demonstrated these changes. Matthew Goldsmith, the rector who had served from 1690 to 1708, was replaced by John Worsley, a member of the leading Island family. A fine stone rectory was built overlooking the church and cottages in the valley. Later in the century the Georgian

rectory at Niton was given a flight of steps to its imposing front door, a clearly visible sign of the superiority of the parish clergyman.

By the 1790s agriculture was thriving. The Napoleonic Wars boosted the Island economy. With many soldiers stationed in town and countryside and continuing demands from the Navy at Portsmouth, the sale of flour and biscuits was guaranteed. Arable cultivation increased and seven or eight times more wheat was harvested than was needed for local consumption. The profits from successful farming allowed farmers to improve their homes, as can be seen in the Georgian facade at Yafford House. But even a modest farmer near Pound Green, Freshwater, could provide his wife with a new parlour and dining room, presenting a neat frontage of central door with windows on each side and a chimney stack on each gable end.

The farmhouse parlour represented new

aspirations towards gentility, a place to display the china and glass which increasing numbers could now afford. At Stone House, Blackwater, an eighteenth panelled parlour includes an elegant display cupboard. Even in smaller farmhouses there was space for pretty curved and fluted alcove shelves. Except in newly built houses upstairs rooms remained much as in the past. Public rooms could be added or adapted, but bedrooms in older houses continued to be entered from each other and the only privacy lay behind the closed curtains of the four-poster bed.

ABOVE Sketch by John Nixon showing the need for curtained beds. Farmhouses and cottages had stairs opening directly into rooms. Bedrooms were entered from one to the next, with no upstairs passage.

In the management of her household two innovations particularly helped the housewife. The first was the domestic pump, which replaced the laborious work of hauling water from the well. Situated in the yard, close to the back door, eighteenth century pumps were superior domestic items, some with the date of their installation moulded into the lead cover, as at Horringford, or with a classical female figure, as on the pump at Gotten Manor, Chale. The second change was the use of coal

BELOW Standen House, Shide. Red brick, the roof concealed behind the parapet, a handsome door and well-placed windows make this house a model of late eighteenth century domestic architecture. Built onto an earlier farmhouse, it was the home of Henry Roberts, a prominent Newport banker, before the financial collapse of his bank ruined him, and many Newport families.

RIGHT God's Providence House, Newport. An older house was brought up-to-date in 1701. The coved door hood, with its scrolled brackets and shell decoration make it the finest doorway in Newport.

OPPOSITE TOP A sketch by John Nixon of the interior of the New Inn, Brighstone, in 1805. The three-legged table stood firmly on the wide, uneven boards. A modern basket grate with hobs replaced the open fire and a deep fender enclosed the hearth.

OPPOSITE BOTTOM Newport High Street at the end of the eighteenth century. John Nixon was sitting under the stone arches of the Butter Market when he painted this scene. The houses are in a transitional stage. The wood-framed houses are already covered with brick or stucco but the unmistakable Tudor jetties remain. The windows have not yet changed from casements to sashes. It is Saturday market day and the farmer's wife, or daughter, has been selling her geese. The soldiers in the street were part of a military force that contributed to Island prosperity at this time.

for cooking and heating, which led to large open, log-burning fireplaces gradually falling out of use. The first coal fires were held in free-standing iron basket grates, but by the end of the century grates were constructed with little hobs on each side of the fire basket and then built into the fireplace wall itself.

It was in the Island towns that these changes were most obvious. Wood and thatch were replaced by brick and tile. Newport, still the largest town in the Island, was transformed, although it still retained the medieval scheme of housing with narrow frontages to the street and long, sometimes spacious gardens at the back. Old houses acquired tiled roofs with deep eaves, classical doorways and sash windows. The narrow space available for some houses meant that the front door opened into a passage with the staircase at the back and a front and back room to one side.

Even smaller houses had doors opening directly into the front room with stairs tucked behind and the kitchen at the back. Shortage of space on the ground floor was often

compensated for by two upper storeys which gave room for a first floor parlour or drawing room.

Double-fronted Georgian houses still remain, particularly in the streets leading down to the harbour where traders and merchants lived. The finest eighteenth century entrance is that of God's Providence House, standing on the corner of Pyle Street and St Thomas's Square. Local tradition associates it with protection from the plague in earlier times and it is certainly earlier than 1701, the date above the doorway. This relates to various alterations, including the addition of the distinctive shell hood over the door.

The transformation of Newport was completed by 1800; it had become a brick and tile town heralding the rebuilding and new building which marked the nineteenth century. Yarmouth, too, changed its face. It was still small at the turn of the century with only 73 houses including cottages, but the older houses were given new roofs, doors and windows, and even today its centre still retains the charm of genteel eighteenth century life. Cowes was developing both as a port and ship-building town and, at the end of the century, as a

ABOVE The House of Industry, Parkhurst.

LEFT Ford Mill House, Newport, built near the harbour, is typical of the neat frontages that transformed eighteenth century towns. Blue-black brick was used for the walls, and the windows were faced in red brick.

fashionable summer resort, though present day Cowes is essentially a nineteenth century creation.

A final outstanding building must be mentioned, the Isle of Wight House of Industry, a vast 'Pauper Palace', built on an elevated site at the eastern end of Parkhurst Forest about a mile from Newport. It was designed to accommodate 600 inmates, the first of whom crossed its threshold in August 1774. The House of Industry was the largest and most expensive rural workhouse of its time, costing between £18,000 and £20,000. But it was well built, the red bricks costing '18/- (90p) per 1000 laid in their proper place', and most of the original building remains today as part of St Mary's Hospital.

FOUR

Three Distinguished Eighteenth Century Houses

Appuldurcombe is undoubtedly the most distinguished house built in the Island. In grandeur of style, in its furnishings and as a museum housing classical antiquities and European paintings of great quality, nothing could compare with it in the eighteenth century.

The estate lay between Godshill and Wroxall and had been at that time the property of the Worsleys for nearly three centuries. A fortuitous marriage brought the Worsleys to the Island when a son of the Yorkshire Worsley family married Ann Leigh, the heiress of Appuldurcombe, in the early years of the sixteenth century. James Worsley when still a boy attended Prince Henry and grew up in the Royal Household. Ann Leigh arrived at court as a lady-in-waiting to Henry VIII's first wife Queen Catherine. The young couple met and by their wedding in 1511 the Isle of Wight Worsleys were established. James Worsley found his royal patron generous in granting to him almost all the official posts in the Island, including those of Captain of the Isle of Wight and Constable of Carisbrooke Castle. And it was James who obtained outright possession of Appuldurcombe, making it from the sixteenth century the site of a handsome house set in the valley around which the estate was centred.

In 1690 Sir Robert Worsley married Frances Thynne of Longleat, but the sixteenth century house was hardly an inviting prospect for the new bride. Prior to his marriage Sir Robert had made a tour of Europe and was well acquainted with the classical style so much admired at that time. He was determined to build a mansion in the most fashionable manner and to remove the old house completely, leaving 'not . . . one stone standing.'

The design of the house was prepared by John James, not a major architect, but a man who had been employed in the King's Works and was to become Assistant Surveyor to Sir Christopher Wren four years after he completed Appuldurcombe. Certainly his skill in interpreting classical form within a country house frame was considerable and resulted in a building unique to the Island.

Work began in 1701 using local greensand and stone from the old Tudor house. By 1711 the splendid east front with its two projecting pavilions was complete, an exotic Baroque intruder in a countryside of simple wood or stone buildings. The ornamental detail was concentrated on the east front entrance, where two skilled London masons transformed Portland stone into elaborate Corinthian capitals, draped fringed swags, bows and tassels of finest delicacy to frame the circular window above the doorway.

Much of the material and labour used in the building came from the estate, but even so by 1711 £3,532 had been expended on the work, a sum not greatly different from the cost of building other large houses at this time. But the expense at Appuldurcombe was sufficient to convince Sir Robert that work must stop, leaving the completion of the house 'to the next age.'

The next age was some time coming as Sir Robert's son had no children and the estate was entailed and held in family trusts. Appuldurcombe's completion was left to Sir Richard Worsley, who succeeded to the estate in 1768. He was ideally suited to the task, having both been on the Grand Tour and married a rich wife, Dorothy Seymour Fleming, thus combining his knowledge and her money to the pleasures of bringing Appuldurcombe up to the standards of the day. One obvious way was to 'improve' the landscape in which the house stood, and so the most fashionable improver of the time, Lancelot 'Capability' Brown, came to Appuldurcombe. He designed a landscape setting which extended a park beyond the old stone-walled deer park to carry the eye upward and outward to a tall stone obelisk dedicated to Sir Robert on Appuldurcombe Down to the west, and to the 'Gothic' ruin, Cook's Castle, on St Martin's Down to the east.

Brown is remembered for his landscapes, but he also designed buildings and recent research suggests that it was he who completed the

The east front of Appuldurcombe, the main residence of the Worsley family in the Island from 1701, when building began, until 1855 when the estate was sold. This front belongs to work undertaken by Sir Robert Worsley between 1701-1711. The right hand pavilion was the dining parlour, the left, the drawing room, separated by the Great Hall. The chimneys were collected in groups to form classical arches, while further classical figures and urns decorated the roof line of the original house. These were later replaced by the present balustrade.

Following the sale of the estate, the house gradually fell into disrepair. By 1932 it was reported as being 'habitable but badly damaged', and it was finally destroyed during the Second World War when a land mine fell nearby.

house, building the northwest pavilion for the kitchen and adding new rooms at the back. However, it was not the additional building or the landscaping that made this remote house famous in its day but rather the remarkable furnishings and art treasures it contained. Just as he chose a fashionable landscape artist Sir Richard commissioned an equally fashionable designer to furnish the most important rooms in the house. Thomas Chippendale's firm undertook the work and we are fortunate that an inventory made between 1779-1781 allows us to visualize the interior of the house as Chippendale conceived it.

Part of the building work in the 1770s included improvements to the hall, the main east front entrance. A marble floor was laid and the ceiling was raised to allow space for eight columns, four at each end, lightly dividing the space into three. Here the colours were cool. Four carved table frames painted grey and white supported tops of scagliola while the cane furniture was green and white. But these were incidentals for here in the main entrance to the house the walls were covered with portraits, mostly of the Worsley family itself, spanning several generations and painted by the greatest artists of each period, including Van Dyck, Lely and Kneller. Joshua Reynolds

Appuldurcombe. This engraving shows the house surrounded by its parkland. Behind it, on Stenbury Down, is a stone obelisk erected in 1774 as a monument to Sir Robert Worsley the builder of Appuldurcombe.

had recently painted companion portraits of Sir Richard and his wife, he wearing the uniform of his regiment and Lady Worsley in a dress which copied the military style of her new husband. The hall was a statement and foretaste of what the house had to offer.

A white and gold drawing room was the most magnificent of the formal rooms. Its walls were lined with white silk woven in alternate stripes of satin and watered silk, with a single curtain of the same material hanging at each of the three windows. The cornice was carved and gilded in burnished gold, as were the two pier tables between the windows. Mirrors were everywhere; gilded pier mirrors above the tables, a very large 'chimney glass' and two other wall mirrors. On the floor lay 'a large Axminster carpet to imitate the Cieling', a feature more often associated with the Adam brothers. Gobelin tapestries hung on the walls. They were copies of paintings at Versailles representing the Arts and Sciences, a very eighteenth century theme. Complementing the wall hangings were eight gilded elbow chairs

and a sofa upholstered in the same tapestry. A bold addition to this room was a set of six cane elbow chairs japanned in red and white with covers and cushions in crimson stripes. Although this strong colour seems intrusive, cane, japan and crimson all introduced a sense of the Orient, which was greatly admired in the eighteenth century.

The 'Dining Parlour' was soberly furnished in mahogany; two circular tables between the three windows with mirrors above them, a sideboard, a wine cooler to hold bottles and a set of twelve chairs with green leather seats. Fashionable pea-green was the colour chosen for the festoon window curtains. Both the name of the room and the absence of a named dining table show that the chairs and tables remained standing against the walls waiting to be brought forward when meals were served. Green was also the library colour; pea-green worsted damask curtains, a painted floor cloth and two very large deal bookcases painted green and white. The few movable pieces of furniture were mahogany, including eight elbow chairs which were designed for a library. The backs were urn-shaped and into them were set Wedgwood plaques of eight authors, four classical - Homer, Aratus, Caesar and Seneca, and four English - Shakespeare, Milton, Locke and Pope.

The work of extending and furnishing Appuldurcombe filled the years of Worsley's short-lived marriage. By 1782 he and his wife were divorced and Sir Richard left to travel in Greece and Turkey, both then dangerous, and from where he returned with important collections of antique marbles. He was an avid collector, and also bought many European paintings, so that his great mansion became more a museum than a home. From 1797 until his death in 1805 Richard Worsley lived mainly in his Sea Villa on the Undercliff, leaving Appuldurcombe to the discerning visitors who were allowed to view the house and its remarkable contents.

Appuldurcombe was unique. No other Island house of the period matched it. But by the time Worsley returned from his travels the formality of classical houses had succumbed to the newer enthusiasm for romantic and dramatic scenery and it was already out of date. The coasts of the Isle of Wight exactly met these needs and architects were ready to create houses to fit such surroundings.

Eighteenth century visitors approaching the Island from Southampton would see ahead of them across the harbour from the little town of Cowes a green and wooded hillside sloping down to the shore, presenting just the picturesque view that made the sea crossing worth while. But in the last years of the century their view was suddenly 'improved' by the building of not one but two castles within a short distance of each other, each of which was built by a major architect.

The first was Norris Castle, begun in 1795 as a seaside residence for Lord Henry Seymour, a wealthy bachelor who could afford to commission James Wyatt, the Surveyor General, to design his new home. Wyatt was already noted for his work on medieval buildings and it was this style he chose for the new castle. Norris is poised on the crest of a hill commanding an important sea passage so Wyatt built an austere stone castle in the Norman style dominated by a great round tower, the whole seen as a magnificent silhouette from the sea. Local stone was used for the external walls, the pointing around each block galletted with tiny fragments of flint. There was also an inner wall of brick and below the castle were cellars, rainwater storage tanks and ice storage pits dug out at a still lower level.

Wyatt put his main rooms in the round tower and between two lower square towers, hiding the roof behind a crenellated wall. But this

The Round Tower, Norris Castle. James Wyatt made this tower the focal point of his romantic medieval castle, giving the house a circular drawing room. The castle was strongly built from local stone, the pointing galletted with tiny flints, a time consuming but attractive detail, which could be afforded by Lord Henry Seymour, a wealthy bachelor.

entrance front, although creating a Gothic effect, was a balanced classical design with a central porch and round-headed windows on each side. The hall led directly to a small terrace looking down to the sea. Its length was broken into three sections by arches and the roof of each was simply vaulted into quarters. The staircase was equally plain, stone treads were cantilevered into the wall and plain iron balusters in groups of three supported the hand rail.

In the public rooms the same austerity was duplicated. The stone fireplaces in the drawing room and dining room were Tudor in style, with the merest Gothic motifs at each lintel corner. The cornices of each room were equally restrained, the drawing room with a dainty floral design, the dining room with a slightly heavier leaf pattern. Wyatt designed a beautifully proportioned drawing room within the round tower, with three large windows looking seaward. This room was set behind the library, which itself was part of the castle frontage. By contriving curved book cupboards Wyatt linked the library with the circular drawing-room, where similar Gothic cupboards were built around the walls. Having placed the main rooms conveniently together Wyatt then extended the castle to create the asymmetrical line of an eighteenth century picturesque building. This section led to a splendid kitchen court flanked by sturdy towers and entrance doors high and wide enough to admit laden wagons.

Norris Castle's towers and crenellated walls alone justify its importance, but it does not stand alone. Visitors entered a Gothic estate from the moment they passed the tall round tower of the entrance lodge. From here the drive curved down to the main castle through pleasant grounds and then rose to pass a more rustic castle some distance on. Behind these long walls, square corner towers and impressive entrance lay the kitchen gardens, stables and farmyard. Norris was completed in 1805 and it remains virtually unaltered today, forming a unique and outstanding contribution to the Island's domestic architecture.

The second eighteenth century castle above East Cowes no longer exists, built over by a modern housing estate, but in its first and most glorious period East Cowes Castle dominated the landscape across the harbour from Cowes. It was only two years after Wyatt began Norris Castle that John Nash began to build his castle on a site adjoining the Norris estate. Both these fashionable architects were patronized by the royal family, Wyatt by George III and his wife, Nash by the Prince Regent, later George IV. Wyatt was appointed Surveyor General in 1796 and after his death Nash succeeded him as architect to the Office of Woods and Forests in 1806.

1798 was a landmark year for John Nash, marking both his marriage and the purchase of his East Cowes estate. His work in building country houses had restored his fortunes, his partnership with the landscape gardener Humphrey Repton was successful and he had met the Prince Regent. To prove his prosperity he now began building his Isle of Wight home on a dramatic site overlooking Cowes harbour. But Nash was a pragmatist, who knew that as wealthy and aristocratic visitors flocked to Cowes they would be confronted by a splendid advertisement to his architectural skills.

The castle in its earliest form was built remarkably quickly. In early December 1802 the *Hampshire Telegraph* reported that Mrs Nash had just given her annual ball and supper, which suggests that this was already an established event. The building work was not as time-consuming as at Norris, the walls went up quickly and an immediate effect was achieved with square castellated towers and a circular staircase tower. Within these were the public rooms, drawing room, dining room and library and there was also a conservatory, an essential feature of country houses at this time.

Within a few years the house increased in size, the most important addition being a massive octagon tower with its own slender staircase tower, a bold addition to this already picturesque castle. Alterations and additions were made by Nash over the years, including extending the conservatory – a large glass building which looked out over gardens which mixed a formal garden complete with fountain with rounded flowerbeds and islands of shrubs set in grass.

In common with Appuldurcombe and Norris Castle visitors were allowed to view Nash's home and we can glimpse the interior from a description by Joseph Farrington in 1817. The round tower which carried the staircase had fluted walls and rose to a domed ceiling decorated in one of Nash's favourite scaly patterns. The drawing room was elegant with doors leading into the conservatory. The deeply curved cornice was decorated with a gilded anthemion pattern, creating another scaly effect. Curved bays at each end of the room had lower flat ceilings and recesses filled with mirrors. A white marble fireplace was supported by two Egyptian figures and French *directoire* furniture completed the decoration, In the dining room the cornice included a tiny decoration of curtains and tassels painted red

East Cowes Castle, the home of John Nash was sited on a hill overlooking Cowes Harbour and clearly visible from the town and the sea. John Nash re-invented medieval architecture in a picturesque style for his castle with a free use of crenellation for his towers and walls. Humphry Repton is believed to have designed these gardens, which show the transition from landscape gardening to informal shrubs and flower beds. The short conservatory was extended later.

and gold above the fluted cove. Here Nash displayed drawings of some of the many houses he had designed. The octagon tower with its eight arches led into a remarkable billiard room with ten small domes surrounding a top light with round-headed arches around the central space. This was the house as theatre, where the effect was more important than

convenience or comfort. Perhaps the best impression of what the interior might have looked like in its early days may be seen by visitors to Buckingham Palace, where the decoration reflects the descriptions given by Farrington.

East Cowes Castle was a house made for entertaining. In August 1815 a grand fête was held in the grounds with marquees for dancing. The Prince Regent dined there in 1817 and towards the end of Nash's life in 1833 Princess Victoria and her mother were entertained to refreshments after attending the consecration of Nash's newly built church of St James in East Cowes, During the following year his health began to fail and by the spring of 1835 he was bedridden. Nash kept up his diary almost to the end, the last entries being very simple, 'very ill, no appetite'. On the 11 May he wrote, 'Cowes - much worse' and two days later he died.

He was buried quickly and quietly at St James's church, and his widow, together with Ann Pennethorne, her cousin and constant companion, moved to Hamstead Lodge, an ancient building near Yarmouth which Nash had bought in 1806 and converted into a cottage *orné*. East Cowes Castle was sold to the Earl of Shannon to help pay off John Nash's debts, later becoming the home of the Gort family.

In the 1930s the castle was showing signs of its age, the war years accelerated the decay and by 1949 the building was beyond viable restoration. The end came in the 1960s when the remaining structure was demolished, the ground cleared and the present modest houses replaced the grand picturesque castle which had enlivened the landscape of East Cowes for nearly a century and a half.

Each of these eighteenth century houses was representative of its period. Appuldurcombe is unique, no other building of such architectural style was built in the Island. Norris Castle in its austere Gothic form is of major importance as an almost unaltered collection of buildings by James Wyatt. John Nash's castle has gone, but in the history of domestic buildings in the Isle of Wight his influence was to continue for many years after his death.

FIVE

The Idea of the Cottage

'The Isle of Wight is full of cottages', remarked an early nineteenth century visitor. He was quite right; agricultural commentators in the late eighteenth century and the Poor Law Commissioner in 1832 all noted the numbers of labourers' cottages. To these must be added the many pretty cottage *ornés* built in this period. Charles Vancouver, surveying the agricultural life of the Island in 1810, found more cottages attached to farms than in other parts of Hampshire, well-built in brick as well as stone on the richer greensand farmlands he visited. On the cold northern clays it was different. Some wood-framed houses with mud walls and thatched roofs survived into the twentieth century before they were swept away and replaced with cheap brick and tile houses. These rural cottages had large gardens, up to two thirds of an acre was considered

Views of eighteenth century kitchens are rare but this scene painted by John Nixon at 'Steepe Hill, Nr Ventnor' shows a homely room with candlesticks on the mantelpiece, cauldron over the fire, with bellows and tongs to hand. The deep fringe of material hanging from the mantelpiece helped the fire to draw. A clothes horse has the washing airing on it.

reasonable for a labourer to cultivate without tiring himself for his farm work. This land was crucial to labouring families. On it they grew potatoes, their staple food, to which they added wheaten bread and small amounts of bacon from the cottage pig. Only minute quantities of tea, sugar and cheese enlivened this bleak diet, which remained the daily fare of labourers in the southern counties from the late eighteenth century until the 1870s, when food prices fell and a more varied diet was possible.

By the middle of the eighteenth century a common type of labourer's cottage had evolved, a simple rectangular building of one room with a large fireplace and a bread oven set into a gable wall. J.L. Whitehead in *The Undercliff of the Isle of Wight* describes the interior of one such cottage in 1911, 'the fireplace being roomy with a small seat on each side. The chimney was wide open. . . An iron bar was fixed across the chimney, and to this a cotterell was fastened or hooked, and to the chain an iron pot or steamer was usually attached.'

Edwin Holbrook of Porchfield has a similar description of the hearth in his grandparents' cottage near Poleclose Farm, Carisbrooke, in the late 1870s. Its mud walls were covered by a deep thatch roof. Small windows with diamond-shaped leaded glass gave little light to the cottage. He, too, describes the iron pot suspended on the cotterell hook in which potatoes in a net, cabbage and a small piece of meat boiled together, exactly as his ancestors had cooked at the beginning of the nineteenth century. His account mentions some of the furnishings in the house; an old oak chest, a highback chair for his grandfather, a dresser with hanging jugs and open shelves on which plates and vegetable dishes stood. A much-prized Dutch striking clock with long chains hung on one wall, while others were decorated with large photographs of Charles Spurgeon,

the most popular non-conformist preacher of his day, Gladstone, John Bright, and Joseph Arch, founder of the Agricultural Labourers' Union. This was a radical household.

The walls of these single-roomed cottages were often up to two feet thick, cut through on one long side for an entrance door. The cottagers used their simple furniture to make the living room as comfortable as possible. A high-back settle would be placed at right angles to the door, creating an entrance passage and diverting some of the draughts. A steep ladder stair led directly into a single upper room where the gable chimney stack rose up to the roof. In Victorian times this family bedroom was partitioned by fastening tall boards to the bedhead, giving parents a modest sense of privacy. These basic houses continued to be built in the early nineteenth century, even though some new-built cottages were already adopting the neat balanced frontages of Georgian England. The drawing of a cottage to be built at Atherfield in 1797 shows this clearly, with its central door and staircase and a chimney at each gable.

Elevation of a proposed cottage to be built at Atherfield in 1797. Chimneys have moved to the gable ends of the house, leaving space for a staircase. A balanced eighteenth century front was possible but the windows remain low casements.

Winkle Street, Calbourne, also known as Barrington Row, after the family who owned the Swainston estate in the eighteenth century. The cottages were built in twos and threes from the second half of the eighteenth century, and are a good example of how a long row of cottages gradually evolved.

Meanwhile, rows of cottages were built during the Georgian period. They had not been unknown earlier but now groups of two or three small houses under one thatched roof were seen in the countryside. Those that can be dated in the Island were built from the late eighteenth century onwards. Some, often those built near or within view of the local manor house, were clearly intended to provide an attractive scene.

Such groupings can be seen at Shorwell opposite one entrance to North Court and at Winkle Street, Calbourne, where the long row of cottages began life in the last quarter of the eighteenth century. Later Victorian cottages were equally pleasing to the eye although the interiors were not.

At the end of Queen Victoria's reign a thatched cottage in Freshwater used one of the bedrooms as a pigsty; a 'still more picturesque cottage' had much of the thatch and all the ceiling in one bedroom missing, 'the owner had built the shanty years before and ever after left it severely alone.' It was a fact of nineteenth century life that labourers lived in old, run-down houses because they were the cheapest to rent. This was the time when many seventeenth century farmhouses were divided into two or three cottages to provide for the growing population. Helen Allingham's charming watercolours have left a record of some of these old cottages in the Island as they were at the end of the nineteenth century, but her accurate eye revealed unmistakable signs of age and decay where cold and damp were commonplace.

John Wilkes, the most radical political agitator in the reign of George III, leased Sandham Cottage from 1786, making it a fashionable villa, from which he looked out onto a virtually empty landscape – one which would later become Sandown.

A Governor's cottage at Steephill. Hans Stanley was appointed Governor of the Isle of Wight in 1764 and immediately built a seaside retreat near St Lawrence. It had a fashionable bowed veranda and was much admired as being in 'the true cottage style'.

None of these practical disadvantages was considered by travellers in the last years of the eighteenth century. They regarded thatched cottages as one component in a landscape made up of woods, seashore and a verdant countryside. With sensibilities awakened by romantic poetry and landscape painting, they saw the English countryside as a new Eden, and the rural cottager and his simple home the embodiment of the virtues of country living. The Isle of Wight was particularly well placed to meet these ideals; the adventure of a sea voyage, picturesque downs and villages, and on the southern shores dramatic cliffs, rocky coves and sweeping bays.

Despite appalling roads over the downs the southern coast was attracting visitors in the 1770s. John Wilkes, the political radical, began visiting Sandham (Sandown) and was sufficiently happy to lease Sandham Cottage in 1786, from where he had views to an almost empty and dramatic bay. His home may have

been called a cottage, but within it Wilkes had one room decorated in the fashionable Tuscan style, complete with a Latin dedication to himself.

Hans Stanley began work at Steephill near St Lawrence even earlier. Shortly after he was appointed Governor of the Isle of Wight in 1764 he was tempted, 'by the singularity of the situation . . . to build a cottage here.' It stood on a ledge of rock near the foot of the Undercliff with views down to the sea and along the cliff to the little church of St Lawrence. It was admired for its situation and elegance and was much visited at the end of the eighteenth century, when one feature in the garden attracted particular comment. 'Just before the window of the west front, a beautiful spring of the most transparent water keeps a large stone basin, in the form of a scallop shell, perpetually full.' This was the admiring comment of H.P. Wyndham in 1783, but later in the century William Gilpin scorned

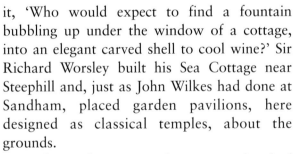

The cottage *orné* at East Cowes designed by John Plaw, as William Cooke saw it in 1808. The great thatched roof followed the Gothic style of the windows and the eighteenth century garden, laid with grass up to the house, was still untouched.

Puckaster Cottage, Niton, was built at some time between 1812-1824. It was designed by Robert Lugar for James Vine, including a fashionable bowed drawing room, with windows looking down to the sea. The thatched roof and veranda still remain.

it, 'Who would expect to find a fountain bubbling up under the window of a cottage, into an elegant carved shell to cool wine?' Sir Richard Worsley built his Sea Cottage near Steephill and, just as John Wilkes had done at Sandham, placed garden pavilions, here designed as classical temples, about the grounds.

By the early nineteenth century thatched cottages for superior families were a feature of island life, as George Brannon's many engravings show. John Nash who designed the prettiest of picturesque cottages added them to the local scene. At Westover, Calbourne, a few remain, including Sweetwater Cottage at the back entrance to the estate, a tiny thatched lodge which fits perfectly into its woodland surroundings. Contrast this with the elegant two-storey version in dressed flint at the front entrance to Westover and one can see how Nash was a master at fitting a building into its surroundings.

Other noted architects worked in the Island. John Plaw who lived at Southampton designed a delightful gentleman's cottage with a great curved rustic veranda opposite John Nash's own entrance lodge to East Cowes Castle. Plaw's cottage is no longer there but part of just such a building remains at Niton Undercliff. Puckaster Cottage, which was built at some time between 1812 and 1814, stands on a ledge looking down to the sea with the Undercliff at its back. It was designed by Robert Lugar, another influential cottage architect, for Mr James Vine and his wife after a local builder had failed to translate sketches from one of Lugar's books into a solid building. This 'cottage' included four reception rooms, six bedrooms and extensive servants' quarters. With its bowed front and deep veranda supported on rustic columns, a French window leading from the drawing room into the garden, it was all that a gentleman might wish for in a seaside residence.

Picturesque thatched cottages continued in use throughout the nineteenth century. The Swan's Nest, Ryde, is similar to Lugar's cottage at Niton and it, too, retains the deep bow and rustic columns.

Another example of a similar house may still be seen in Ryde where the Swan's Nest stands among later Victorian houses as an exotic reminder of the town's genteel past. Despite the lavish space within these cottages they remained externally relatively simple when they were first built, retaining something of the modest labourers' and fishermen's cottages on which they were based. Shanklin still has examples of both, in and around the old village, most notably Vernon Cottage, which was built in 1817 and remains an attractive

example of the picturesque cottage.

By the 1820s the simple thatched cottage was being overtaken by a more ornate style where the architect chose to introduce medieval and Tudor features. Puckaster Cottage adopted a Tudor domestic style with deep bargeboards below the roofline. Yaverland Parsonage was built in this Tudor-Gothic style with pointed gables, pointed porch entrance and stone crenellation topping the walls. Lisle Combe at St Lawrence, built for Charles Pelham, second son of Lord Yarborough, was greatly enlarged, making the roof the most distinctive part of the house with tall chimneys, little gabled roofs and windows extending into the roof line, all emphasized with deep, elaborate bargeboards.

Tucked away at the top of Shanklin Chine is

ABOVE Vernon Cottage, Shanklin, engraved in 1831 showing the elaboration which gradually transformed the eighteenth century gentleman's cottage into a nineteenth century cottage *orné*.

ABOVE LEFT Yaverland Parsonage, with its Gothic porch, steep gables and crenellation topping the walls, is a fine example, still surviving, of a romantic clergy house.

LEFT Rylstone Manor, Shanklin. When Rylstone was built it was a new house built between the top of the Chine and the steep cliff. This stone house uses Tudor dripstones, a medieval beamed jetty and elaborate chimneys in a nineteenth century style to fit a romantic landscape.

the present Rylstone Manor, originally a romantic cliff top house. Here elaborate chimneys, gabled roofs and fancy bargeboards made this a perfect picturesque house positioned between the deep gorge and plunging cliff. Bonchurch was a small village which was overtaken in the 1830s by well-to-do families who bought up older houses and built lavish seaside residences. East Dene, the birthplace of Charles Swinburne, was one, Undermount changed from a thatched cottage to a much larger house and Winterbourne, where Charles Dickens stayed for some

months, was another of these fanciful residences.

These rustic or seaside houses originated in the English farmhouse or cottage, but foreign sources also had an appeal. In the Island there are two good examples of the Swiss cottage. The more famous is that at Osborne House which was given to the royal children on Queen Victoria's birthday in 1854. The wooden chalet with its balcony and wide eaves fits well into a woodland setting, with a natural meadow sprinkled with wild flowers in the late spring below it. It also has real Swiss

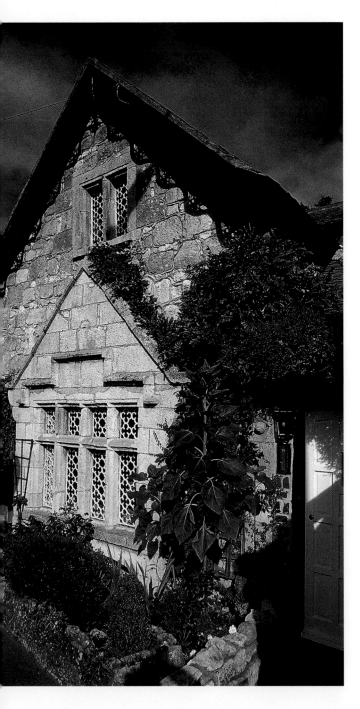

Debourne Lodge, the main entrance to Northwood Park. Here Tudor and classical elements were used to create a picturesque cottage. Both this lodge and the Round House, were probably designed by George Repton, who worked in John Nash's office in the early years of the nineteenth century.

a suite of furniture made in golden American birch has bobbin-turned legs and dainty chair backs in open scroll work, all suitable for a Swiss cottage but made in Newport by Francis Pittis in 1854.

The second Swiss cottage was built in the grounds of Rylstone Manor and is more typical of the English style of these houses. It is a good stone building with a wooden balcony, ornamented bargeboards and simple gothic doors and windows. But here the principle of a building fitting its surroundings was completely lost and we have a Swiss cottage on a cliff top facing the English Channel!

The idea of the cottage was never given up. As the nineteenth century advanced industrialization and urban growth gave to cottage life that quality of innocence and simplicity which led the first aristocratic cottage builders to the country and the coast. The idea was a dream, and had no relation to real cottage life, but it retained its hold on the imagination of English people into the twentieth century, since when its influence has been pervasive, despite the fact that two centuries have passed since the fashion for 'gentlemen's cottages' first started.

associations, although the building was probably made on the estate. Prince Albert intended the children to have a practical education drawing on the principles of Pestalozzi, the Swiss educational reformer, and it was here they learned to garden, cook and housekeep. In the dining room on the first floor

SIX

Regency Style

'A very few years ago [Sanditon] had been a quiet village . . . but some natural advantages in its position . . . the probability of it becoming a profitable speculation . . . raised it to something of young renown.' Jane Austen was writing of a fictional town in her unfinished novel *Sanditon*, but she might have written in the same way of Ryde, although here she would have found two quiet villages, one coastal and the other a collection of cottages and farms at the top of a steep rise. But the impetus was the same. By the early years of the nineteenth century seabathing was competing with spa waters in attracting fashionable society, and it was in these emerging nineteenth century towns that Regency elegance in building was to be found.

By 1817 Ryde had already begun its advance to fashionable status. The prospect of a 'profitable speculation' had spurred Jane Player, the ground landlord, to spend money in 1810 on a private Act of Parliament, which allowed her to grant building leases on her property, including the two villages and the surrounding land. Immediately there were applications for ninety-year leases. The first Marquis of Buckingham leased a site where the land ran down to the sea in 1812 and within a

Buckingham House, Ryde, the seaside residence of the first Duke of Buckingham, was built by 1813. This villa, and its owner, indicate the social standing of those who built houses on the west side of Union Street in the early nineteenth century. The garden frontage, seen here, is little altered today.

Westfield House was the Ryde home of the 2nd Earl Spencer and his family. It stood on a rise with gardens sweeping down to the shore. This early nineteenth century villa was given a distinctive 'Osborne Tower' later in the century.

In 1843 August Clifford bought Westfield House. He employed Thomas Hellyer, a Ryde architect, to add a sculpture gallery to the villa. The gallery is seen here in the 1930s when it was used as a ballroom in Westfield Hotel.

year his son, the first Duke, was able to move into a large villa with four ground floor bay windows facing seawards. In 1818 the neat Marine Villa with its spacious garden was built nearby for a London purchaser, whilst further to the west, on an elevated site overlooking the sea, Westfield House was built as a large square villa with extensive grounds sloping down to the shore. This became the seaside residence of the 2nd Earl Spencer and his family. These examples of the earliest development of Ryde

are typical in showing that mainland wealth formed the corner-stone of much of the new building.

The Player family made its own contribution. George Player, who had inherited Ryde Farm, built Ryde House for himself in 1810, setting it in fields towards Binstead and converting the farmland into a landscape park. A few years later Dr John Lind and his wife Elizabeth, daughter of Jane Player, built their elegant villa, Westmont, now Ryde School, a short distance away. Mrs Lind laid the foundation stone in 1819 and by the autumn of 1821 she was able to write, 'Dr Lind and I slept for the first time in our new house.'

These detached early villas conform to a basic plan which remained a practical form of house well into the nineteenth century. The requirements were simple; an entrance hall with an elegant staircase, a drawing room and dining room on each side, a library or morning

ABOVE George Player built Ryde House for himself in 1810 when he inherited Ryde Farm. The fields became a landscape park surrounding his villa. The north front still retains the iron balcony.

BELOW Westmont is a Regency villa built by Doctor and Mrs Lind in 1819. Mrs Lind was the daughter of Jane Player, who stimulated the development of Ryde by granting building leases on her land. Westmont is now the core of Ryde School, a fine example of Regency elegance. It included a laundry, brewhouse, cow stalls and a walled kitchen garden, demonstrating the self-sufficiency of gentlemen's houses.

Cowes was already fashionable by the opening years of the nineteenth century, attracting aristocratic families in the sailing season. Belmore House, the seaside villa of the Earl of Belmore was completed in 1811. It was built close to the shore and the classical facade hides a wood frame which allows the house to adapt to movement in the ground. It was painted pink when it was first built and retains that colour today, standing out clearly when seen from the sea.

room set behind the drawing room, connected by wide central doors which turned the two reception rooms into one for special occasions. The kitchen behind the dining room was the living room for the cook and maids who squeezed into small rooms under the eaves when they finally fell into bed. In such towns as Ryde, Buckingham House and Marine Villa were not family homes, they were seasonal houses, bases from where the visiting families took part in the many social engagements a fashionable seaside town offered.

The earliest villas were built in a Georgian style but were lighter in material and detail. One example of this transition is found at Cowes which, like Ryde, was also adapting to fashionable visitors. In what is now Queens Road the first house built on this stretch of coast was completed in 1811. It was to be the seaside residence of the Earl of Belmore, whose family seat was in distant County Fermanagh. The structure was a wood frame with lath and plaster infilling set directly on the ground so that the lightly built house was capable of some movement. A severely plain frontage with two sets of windows on each side of a pillared porch and the raised wall with a deep frieze hiding the roof line are virtually unaltered from the time of building. The stucco facing was painted pink from its earliest days and this solitary house with its garden running down to the strand must have been a notable landmark to the many vessels heading into Cowes.

The tradition of building in wood had continued throughout the eighteenth century, especially in the construction of farm buildings using weatherboarding over a wood frame. At the end of the century and during the Regency period weatherboard was used in the southern counties for small cottages and sometimes larger villas. In this way builders avoided paying Brick Tax, which had increased markedly during the Napoleonic wars. Domestic buildings of this type are rare in the Island but a few small cottages remain in Newport, while at Cowes a large corner house can be seen in Bath Road. A weatherboard villa with a veranda still stands in Castle Road, Newport, one of the earliest nineteenth century houses to be built on open space between Newport and Carisbrooke.

Westover, Calbourne, was the home of Sir Leonard Troughear Holmes. This view drawn by Brannon in 1822 shows the Regency house which replaced an eighteenth century 'hunting box'. John Nash designed it, together with the entrance lodges and other estate cottages. The classical features used to create this elegant house were adapted by small builders for the villas and cottages they were building in the Island at this time.

Cement stucco, was the fashionable facing material for genteel houses, a reaction to the plain brick frontages of eighteenth century houses. Stucco over brick could give an appearance of stone and when painted lightened the whole appearance of a building. The great exponent of stucco was John Nash, 'who found us all brick and leaves us all plaster'. His classical country houses and brilliant townscapes in London were to influence builder-developers throughout the country. In the Island one outstanding country house remains where we can see his skill in handling classical themes with delicacy and panache.

At Westover, Calbourne, Nash was employed to transform the eighteenth century house into a fashionable Regency home for a new bride. In 1813 Leonard Troughear Holmes married Anne Delgarno and in the same year work began on the house and lodges. The old house was subsumed into the new building, in which could be seen the Regency details speculative builders adopted for their more modest dwellings. The entrance front has beautifully

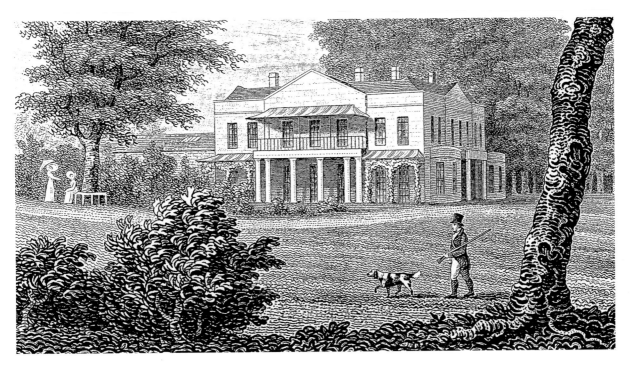

53

placed sash windows, a porch supported on classical pillars, a deep, plain frieze hiding the roof line and a triangular pediment as the central feature of the frontage. All very Georgian, but the effect is softened by single-storey curved bays on each side of the entrance, simple and graceful innovations that transform the building. The garden front repeats the basic classical features, but here a pillared veranda shades the rooms facing south and creates an informal link between the house and garden.

Practical developments in building techniques contributed to this effect. Shallow pitched roofs were made possible by the use of thin Welsh slate, glazing bars in windows were skilfully cut to narrow half inch dimensions. Increasingly common imported softwoods had to be protected from the weather and so windows, doorcases and weatherboarding received coats of white lead paint, all contributing to a bright exterior.

The external shapes of villas changed as curved lines replaced, or were added to, straight walls. Curved bays became features of drawing rooms, as at Westover, and were sometimes extended through two storeys, seen today in a fine house standing in The Mall, Brading. Simultaneously, houses were being adorned with decorative wrought iron work; foliage, flowers, geometric forms, Chinese fretwork, Gothic arches, all could be selected for balconies, which were increasingly fashionable. Lind Street, Ryde, still has balconied houses in this style built for middle class families to rent. When this street began to be developed in the 1830s Ryde had already achieved the status of a town. Between 1811 and 1831 nearly three hundred houses were built for the rapidly growing population. Many of them remain, well repaired and maintained, making Ryde the best Regency town in the Island.

Ryde was not alone in acquiring fashionable airs and graces. Farther to the east the little village of Bembridge was from 1826 being 'improved' by a local developer, Edward Wise. Most notably he took an old farmhouse and had it transformed by John Nash into Hill Grove, a magnificent Regency house with a central dome and fine classical adornments. It became the residence of the Earl of Ducie and remained the family home of the Reynolds-Moretons who were so influential in Bembridge life in the nineteenth century. Hill Grove dominated the wooded hill overlooking the harbour, while more modest villas were built in what was to be the centre of the village. Bembridge parish was detached from Brading in 1827 and its chapel of ease was built, later to be replaced by a parish church. The village grew around the church and parsonage where today a group of plain Regency villas remain, with shallow roofs and neat sash windows, comfortable homes in a village which was from the beginning a superior place in which to live.

At Cowes a major building project was undertaken in the 1830s when the second George Ward replaced Bellevue House with a new house and laid out a large park around it. Northwood House, as it was renamed, had all the external features of a Regency building, stucco finished in a rusticated style on the ground floor, classical pediments, the roof hidden by balustrading, a two storey bay facing the sea. It must then have been a handsome sight. But families will insist on 'improving' their homes and in the 1840s the house was extensively enlarged, including the addition of a circular hall with a large dome at the north west end. The final result was a strangely unbalanced building in which individual features look right but the whole does not create a unity.

At a lower level of society the demand for houses quickened pace. For them a new housing style was introduced early in the century. When John Nash produced his designs for Regent's Park he included houses for all

J. Nixon's Bed-room at Ryde

John Nixon's view of his bedroom at Ryde. The wallpaper was laid onto panels and pinned to the walls. The design is a fashionable eighteenth century theme, the trees suggesting an Indian or Far East location. The festoon curtains and basket grate are typical of this period. Note the boats framed in the window.

sections of society, including semi-detached villas for men of modest means but with pretensions to style. Pairs of cottages were common as labourers' homes in the country, but Nash built pairs of stucco villas which appeared to be one elegant building. It was a housing style which met the needs of the time and where Nash led local builders were not slow to follow. A pleasing group of semi-detached stone houses still stands in Terrace Road, Newport, an early nineteenth century development designed to attract middle class families. In these houses much is made of the bays which run the whole height of the frontage. They follow the pattern of the bays

used in 1812 at Buckingham House, Ryde, with large front windows and two side lights at right angles to them. These plain windows could be filled with cheap manufactured glass, whereas curved sashes still needed panes made to fit their particular dimensions.

Inside these Regency houses decoration was refined to the minimum. Fireplace surrounds were plain with the simplest decoration, a square or circle at the angle of the uprights which were themselves undecorated, as were the iron grates now built into the chimney space. Staircases continued this simple theme, with slender iron or wooden balusters and a narrow wood handrail finished with a curved scroll. Interior walls, however, lost their pristine plaster finish as wallpaper covered them from dado to picture rail. In older houses fashion demanded that old panelling should go. At Nunwell John Nash recommended removing the earlier panelling, replacing it with wallpaper. In the eighteenth century drawing

room, now the library, a new paper bought in 1833 still survives in part today, the strong turquoise blue and gold colouring designed to fit the rich eighteenth century decoration. During that year the whole house was refurbished with new furniture and fabrics, as Fanny Oglander described in a letter to her brother, 'Dear Nunwell is to have new furnishings . . . linen called chintz . . . coloured flowers and stripes of blue on a white ground.' All very fashionable, and an indication of the fabrics which the early Victorians would enjoy.

The most important house to be built in the Isle of Wight during the nineteenth century was Queen Victoria's and Prince Albert's coastal retreat at East Cowes, Osborne House. The foundation stone of their own home at Osborne, the Pavilion, was laid on the 23 June 1845, cemented and hammered into place by the royal parents and their two eldest children. Fifteen months later the family moved into their new home. The Pavilion was a triumph for Prince Albert and Thomas Cubitt, the

This view of Osborne shows the completed building with the large Household wing on the right and the Durbar wing on the left. The central portion with its tower was the Pavilion, the home of the Royal Family, a small part of the whole. Thomas Cubitt built a fire-proof house, using cast iron, cement and brick, with a deep layer of crushed shell between each floor. The Pavilion cost £18,000, a carefully costed house, as the Osborne estate and all the building was paid for by Queen Victoria and Prince Albert from their own income.

builder-contractor who worked with the Prince on the design of the Italianate villa, which stood on high ground overlooking Osborne Bay. In choosing Cubitt to direct the works Prince Albert turned his back on eighteenth century individual contracts for bricklaying, joinery, plastering and the many crafts involved in constructing a house. Economy and value for money were essential to the Royal Family, who were building Osborne with their own money. Cubitt offered a fixed price contract, completion on time and his own highly efficient works on the Isle of Dogs where craftsmen could deal with every aspect of building work.

Although ahead of his time as a contractor, much of Cubitt's career had taken place during the Regency period. He brought to Osborne much of that tradition, but combined it with a modern construction of brick arches and cast iron girders. These two elements explain why Osborne House, with all its classical, Italianate style, does, unlike Northwood House, look forward into the nineteenth century. From it emerged a new type of middle class villa in which the 'Osborne tower' was an important feature. Happily, some of these still remain in the Island. At Westfield House the Clifford family added a tower in the mid-nineteenth century. St Gregory in Church Road, Binstead, retains its tower, whilst smaller villas in the Victorian development of Ryde include this distinctive Osborne feature.

If the exterior of the Pavilion has links with the classical past the furnishing of the house was of its own period, much of it designed by Henry Whitaker, a fashionable Victorian designer. The saloon and the dining room were necessarily formal but in the family rooms on the first floor the Queen and Prince Albert could enjoy their personal tastes. The Queen's sitting room captures the essence of Victorian home life, an exuberantly patterned carpet, flowery chintz curtains and a clutter of pictures and photographs. This was a safe haven, a place secure from the world. It encapsulates all that Victorian England looked for in homes throughout the land.

SEVEN

The Victorian Home – Middle Class Morality

Queen Victoria's life encompassed virtually the whole of the nineteenth century. Her name evokes a quality of life which was distinctive in thought and style, and whose influence was felt throughout a vast and expanding empire. The growth in population – in 1801 just under nine million people in England and Wales, by 1911 thirty six million – and the movement of people from the countryside to urban areas transformed our national life. Green fields were invaded by rows of bricks as terraces, semi-detached houses and individual villas marched into the countryside, invading old villages and extending town boundaries far beyond their original margins.

In the early years of Victoria's reign the remnants of classical Regency style and the picturesque eighteenth century lingered on. St John's Parsonage at Newport was built in 1851 some distance from the church in fields at the southern end of Watergate Road. It was a pretty brick house with an asymmetrical frontage, decorative bargeboards and a modestly Gothic front door, continuing the romantic tradition.

The tollhouse at St Lawrence, built six years later, takes its inspiration from Nash's octagonal tower in the front lodge at Westover. In Rookley three neat brick villas were built in the 1860s; they all have shallow roofs, with bargeboards and Gothic front doors and are really Regency villas dressed up with Gothic additions. All were very different from the then fashionable idea of the romantic past, which drew on Sir Walter Scott's novels, medieval buildings, Tudor and Jacobean houses, and styles loosely based on the Italian Renaissance villa.

In the Isle of Wight this eclecticism was concentrated in a major development intended to transform East Cowes into a fashionable village. George Eyre Brooks, a London land agent, was the head of a company which planned to lay out a sloping site at Shamblers Farm as East Cowes Park. By 1843 the ground

The Toll House, St Lawrence, is an example of borrowing from an earlier style. The tower is similar to John Nash's entrance lodge at Westover.

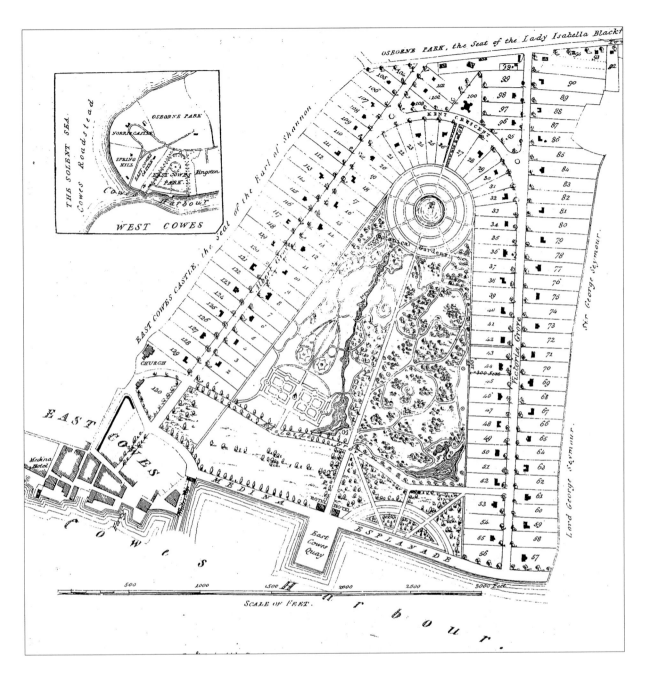

A plan of East Cowes Park, a speculative development in East Cowes in the 1840s. This hippodrome plan of avenues allowed many of the plots to back onto the Botanic Gardens, with a sunken ha-ha seeming to extend their grounds still farther. George Eyre Brooks, the developer, planned over one hundred houses in a variety of styles for the site but the scheme was never fulfilled and the estate was sold in 1874.

had been marked out in a hippodrome shape with botanic gardens as a central feature, separated from the house plots by a deep ha-ha. The company prospectus gave great scope to would-be purchasers; 'They may choose their own designs from a number which have been prepared and which may be altered to suit their convenience.' The sketches of these villas show them to be truly individual in style,

A pair of concrete cottage villas built in East Cowes in 1852. 'Upper Park Cottages', as they were known when built, have solid concrete walls. The houses remain, with later brick additions, and are among the earliest examples in Britain of concrete used in domestic buildings.

miniature medieval castles, gabled Tudor houses, cottages with verandas, and classical villas, all could be supplied. The scheme was grandiose but not without some foundation to encourage the speculators. From 1840 there was a direct railway from London to Southampton and Cowes was already a recognized summer resort of the aristocracy.

A few of these speculative houses have survived to show how the prospective sketches were realized. Victoria Cottage, at the top of York Avenue, boasts a decorative wooden balcony, pierced and scalloped, on what was the back of the building. This was where Thomas Cubitt stayed when he was supervising the work on Osborne House. In 1851 Queen Victoria bought it into the Osborne Estate. Two survivors in the Tudor domestic style are Kent House, originally Powliss House, and Powys House, while two classical villas still stand near Osborne House.

Two houses were particularly innovative. In 1852 Richard Langley leased a site in York Avenue on which to build a pair of 'cottage villas'. He used a new technique, shuttered concrete, to build the external walls. This method allowed him to erect walls of quick drying cement made by the Medina Cement Company, a pioneer in making cement concrete. Langley's cottages stand today as examples of the earliest use of shuttered concrete buildings in Britain.

The prospect of raising money by developing a middle class estate was still being attempted in the 1850s. This time it was a wholly local project. The Simeon family, who owned much of the land east of Ryde, embarked on creating a new park, St John's, on sloping ground near the sea. Thomas Hellyer was employed as architect-designer of a scheme which followed

This view of Osborne shows, on the left, the distinctive tower on the Pavilion which was to be the inspiration for many Victorian villas throughout the Empire. The much larger Household Wing with the Clock Tower is to the right. The villas below Osborne were part of East Cowes Park.

the East Cowes plan of a central garden surrounded by spacious building plots. Today the site can be seen on the ground, a tapered oval, bounded by East Hill and West Hill roads, separated by a wood which has engulfed the garden. Here, too, clients could select the type of house they wanted, or could afford. From those remaining today the ideal seems to have been a Cubitt type villa of three storeys above a basement, and they proved to be attractive to middle class families. An unusual aspect of the development was the provision of houses for outdoor staff in Hill Street, some distance away. Although St John's was more successful than that at East Cowes the estate was sold in 1865 and the remaining land was divided into smaller plots than had been

originally intended. In 1874 East Cowes Park suffered the same fate as it failed to attract middle class clients, ending the first attempts to create garden villages in the Island.

The influence of Osborne House on architectural style was pervasive in the Island, not only the distinctive tower, but the general Italianate features of the house. Wherever there was sufficient money it was possible to imitate the monarch. Shanklin has elegant detached villas in this style in the appropriately named Victoria Avenue, and at Sandford House, Godsill, a large detached villa shows how well the style adapted to later buildings.

It is difficult to think of the Victorians without thinking of the middle classes. They were not the largest section of society, in 1851 they probably accounted for 15% of the population and were no more than 20% by 1900, but they were the most influential. Middle class values of respectability, morality and propriety filtered into all levels of society and ultimately determined what the Victorian

Barton Manor was a successful restoration undertaken by Thomas Cubitt as part of his work on the Osborne estate. The decayed manor house was reduced in size but great care was taken to retain the character of the seventeenth century building. One chimney stack remained in good condition to be used as a pattern for new chimneys.

home should be. As Augustus Pugin, the great advocate of the moral qualities he saw in medieval architecture, emphasized, 'every person lodged as becomes his station'. John Ruskin, possibly the most important thinker and writer on the values behind Victorian building, wrote of the home, '. . . it is the place of Peace; the shelter.' These two statements were the bedrock on which middle class homes were built in the second half of the century.

Who was this new social class whose influence was so disproportionate to its numbers? Well-to-do higher civil servants, professional men, successful businessmen and manufacturers could be included at the top end; minor clerks, non-conformist ministers and small independent tradesmen might just make it into the lower levels. The easiest way to recognize a middle class household was to know that it could afford at least one living-in servant. But it was the attitude to the home that counted. As the century advanced 'the hearth and home' became increasingly central to family life, including the father and breadwinner.

To see some of the best Victorian Gothic houses we must return to the Osborne Estate, not because its architecture was much copied in the Island – it was too expensive to build – but because it introduced details which local builders adapted to their own use. The idea of each being lodged according to status was followed by Thomas Cubitt. He began with Barton Manor, where Prince Albert's model farm was to be built. Half the crumbling fifty-seven rooms were knocked down, leaving a generous-sized house to accommodate family and friends of the Royal Family. The tall brick chimneys with their oversailing tops were a major feature of the house. One of the stacks remained in good condition to serve as a pattern for those to be rebuilt. It was carefully surveyed, each brick was measured and new ones were moulded to the same shape and thickness as the originals. This detailed care was extended to the whole building, thus achieving a successful and sympathetic restoration.

The appearance of the manor house determined that of the new farmhouse, which was to stand close by. This was built in stone in Tudor domestic style and was a handsome building reflecting the status of its occupant, the estate steward who supervised nine hundred acres and eighty-four estate workers. In 1855 a new farmhouse was built at Alverstone near Whippingham, where there were no artistic restrictions. The whole farmstead was built in red brick, fired in the brickyard opened across the road. A simple Italianate style was used with deep eaves and round-headed windows on each side of a grand entrance porch. Nearby was the bailiff's house, smaller and simpler but with the same deep eaves and stone string course. Next came the farm workers, whose cottages were sufficiently plainer to establish their position in the estate hierarchy.

In 1870 a new farmhouse was built at Whippingham. Standing alone in an elevated position, Heathfield farmhouse is a model example of a house of this period. Its architect,

One of a pair of Victorian model workers' cottages at East Cowes showing banded brickwork, ground floor casements and round-headed windows. Only estates such as Osborne could afford to build cottages of this quality.

Albert Jenkins Humbert, had already supervised the rebuilding of Whippingham church and was later to design Sandringham House, Norfolk. For Heathfield he used red and yellow bricks. Yellow bricks arched over the windows and were used to create a dogtooth string course as well as horizontal banding in the walls. The red tiled roof was decorated with horizontal patterns of darker tiles. Deep carved bargeboards completed a house that was a fine example of the newest building style.

Simultaneously, a pair of model estate workers' cottages was built in Newbarn Road, East Cowes, using the same combination of red and yellow brick. They have rather more yellow brick banding in the walls and the windows are surmounted with yellow, red and black bricks. Both Heathfield farmhouse and these high quality cottages could only have

been built by a wealthy estate. Most local builders could not afford to match such standards, but they used the ideas – not always so successfully – in the houses they built.

One other estate did create a new community in the 1860s which has survived successfully to this day. Alverstone village, lying between Brading and Newchurch, was newly built on the estate of Richard Webster, Lord Alverstone. His hunting lodge was partnered by pairs of workers' cottages built in red brick with yellow brick quoins and banding in the walls, finished with a date stone and a sweeping W to identify the owner. These houses are more prosaic than those at Osborne, but they reflect more accurately how coloured brick was then used in the Island.

Further east, on the Nunwell estate at Brading, a new house for a senior estate worker was built in the 1860s. Little Hardingshute, was a copybook example of an estate house with its steep gabled roofs, a brick string course and large casement windows. In

Brighstone Rectory was brought up-to-date in the 1840s by the Reverend Edward McAll. The plain eighteenth century wall was given an elaborate Gothic entrance porch. Gothic arches were also added to the ground floor hall and stairway.

1871 it was the home of the estate gamekeeper Charles Ballard, who lived there with his wife and six children.

Solid Victorian housing was not just the prerogative of the country landowner or speculative developer. The number of parishes increased throughout the nineteenth century and new churches meant new clergy houses. In older parishes many clergymen were altering, enlarging, or moving into new and grander houses. In the first half of the century the cost of building usually had to be met by the incumbent himself. This was so in Brighstone where the old rectory was improved in the 1840s by the rector, Edward McAll. The house was already a far cry from the seventeenth century rectory where Thomas Ken, later

In 1833 the entrance front of Calbourne Rectory was rebuilt in the Tudor domestic style. The choice was appropriate to a clergy house of this period, combining propriety and romance in nice proportions. It remains today a picture book example of this style.

Bishop of Bath and Wells, had begun each day with his morning hymn, 'Awake my soul and with the sun thy daily course of duty run'. In the eighteenth century a plain brick wall with sash windows had brought the garden front up-to-date, but by the 1840s it was old-fashioned. McAll added an elaborate Gothic stone porch onto the Georgian front, with long, narrow lancet windows and a crenellated roof line. This opened into a large pillared hall, whose walls were covered with wood panelling almost certainly removed from Ken's own room in the oldest part of the house. At the end of the hall a wide staircase rose beneath a new Gothic arch on which was painted 'Think and Thank', a salutary text to remind the family of their duty as they descended to breakfast each

day. In this parish the rector built cheaply and for effect, but even so his work stretched his resources to the limit. Following his death his widow was obliged to live in one of the small cottages near the church.

Calbourne rectory was rebuilt in 1833, at the beginning of Thomas Woodruffe's incumbency. The old, and very large, house, was given a complete new frontage in Tudor domestic style, with clean cut dripstones, Gothic windows and an entrance which united the front door and two lancet windows under a single dripstone. The work on the house cost one thousand pounds and it remains today a picture book example of an early nineteenth century rectory.

The best example of the unity Victorians looked for in parish life is found at Bembridge where church, school and vicarage are grouped together. The parish was detached from Brading in 1827 and was from the outset blessed with well-to-do vicars. The first vicarage, built in 1829 in the usual brick and stucco, was demolished in the early 1860s to

ABOVE Bembridge Vicarage. The church, vicarage and school were the centre of Victorian village life. In Bembridge this architectural grouping remains, although the school is now the library.

BELOW The Lodge, Mountjoy Cemetery, Carisbrooke. Although this is the entrance to a cemetery the design of this cottage uses so many Gothic features in a small building that it becomes a fantasy in stone.

The Priory, Carisbrooke, photographed shortly after it was built in 1865-66. The Priory of Our Lady of Reparation and St Dominic began life in December 1866 when the first nuns entered the new building designed by Gilbert Blount. The oriel window on the left was the sitting room of Elizabeth, Dowager Countess of Clare, who built the Priory. The order of contemplative nuns remained at Carisbrooke until 1989. The Priory is now the home of Carisbrooke Priory Trust, a centre of Christian healing for those with mental and emotional needs.

make way for the present house. This was probably built in 1862, although an obscure date stone of 1874 suggests later work. The earlier date has some credence as it just pre-dates the marriage of the vicar, the Honourable John Le Mesurier, in 1863. The Ecclesiastical Commissioners' stipulations for clergy houses included a drawing room, dining room and study, each not less than thirteen feet by fourteen feet, a kitchen, scullery, pantry, and larder, a minimum of five bedrooms, a linen closet, a WC and a wine and beer cellar. All these were included in this large house, emphasizing the superior standing of the Anglican clergyman. But many vicarages had to house large families and servants and some clergymen took in boarding pupils, as did Canon Le Mesurier. The vicar's study overlooked both church and school, reinforcing the all-seeing eye of the local clergyman. Bembridge vicarage is still central to the village. It is an outstanding house with its steep gable roof, tall chimneys and stone bay window with Gothic tracery lighting the drawing room. The tone of the house was set in the entrance porch where, above the door, was a verse from Psalm 21, '*Introitum Tuum et Exitum Tuum custodiat Dominum*' ('The Lord shall preserve thy going out and coming in'). The use of Latin established the status and authority of the Victorian clergyman, but it also demonstrated the social gulf which isolated him from most of his parishioners.

To find Victorian Gothic at its most

exuberant we have to trace the influence of the church into the landscape of burial and cemeteries. New municipal cemeteries had to be created as old graveyards were filled. In Newport one was placed on the east side of the Medina while another site was on the slopes of Mountjoy, overlooking Carisbrooke. Newport cemetery has a yellow brick entrance lodge, with turrets, gables, and arches. The lodge at Mountjoy has walls of small stones fitted together like a jig-saw puzzle, held in place by solid stone quoins. A steep roof covers the porch with its pointed entrance arch, and beside it a bay window similar to that at Bembridge vicarage completes a building which combines the ecclesiastical with the domestic in the most fanciful manner.

Middle class houses were more than living spaces. They were seen as refuges from the increasing pressure of the outside world. John Ruskin encapsulated the ideal, '. . . a temple of the hearth watched over by Household Gods.' The home was a closed moral unity, a secure place to which father returned from work, where mother created the ordered life of a

A Victorian parlour at Staplers Road, Newport. The horseshoe fireplace, piano and needlework table were conventional items in a middle class home and the large patterns on the carpet and wallpaper are found in homes from the 1870s.

happy home. Walls, fences, thick shrubberies, even the ivy and Virginia creeper on the house walls, were barriers behind which the household functioned. Mass production allowed rooms to be filled with furniture and decorative trifles, servants were needed to keep all clean and polished. The number of servants was calculated to each level of income and houses were arranged so that they did not intrude on family life. Below stairs, green baize doors and narrow back staircases helped stress the boundaries between master and servant. Even small households could manage this separation as maids rose early to prepare the rooms for the day. Where there was only one staircase servants and family did not need to meet on it as their timetables were quite separate.

The kitchen was the workplace of the house, with its scullery, pantry and larder. Three items

The Victorian kitchener at Carisbrooke Castle. The kitchener stove was first produced in the 1840s and became the symbol of the Victorian kitchen. In its final form it was an efficient system of baking and roasting, providing hot water and boiling plates, all with heat from the central coal fire. The kitchener in which meals were prepared for Princess Beatrice was 6ft long with large ovens, but kitcheners were adapted to fit any size of household.

were essential to it, the built-in dresser, a large table and the coal-fired range. This demanded the closest attention from the earliest hours when the ashes were raked out, the flues brushed, the ovens cleaned, the whole monster blackleaded and any steel fitments burnished before the new fire was lit and cook came down for the day. The Victorian kitchener had advantages compared with earlier methods of cooking. The enclosed heat could provide for one or two ovens and a hot water boiler, with saucepans boiling on top. The range at Carisbrooke Castle was six feet long with a roasting and baking oven each side of the fire and a hot water heater. Smaller, and more sophisticated versions, would have been found in many middle class houses.

While the morality and taste of the detached Victorian villa set a standard, only a minority of people could afford such homes and most would find themselves living in semi-detached or terrace houses. These were to be the real survivors of Victorian housing, adapting to the twentieth century and still providing comfortable family homes.

EIGHT

The Terrace House – an Affordable Home

The nineteenth was the great century for terrace houses. Beginning with John Nash's dramatic frontages in London they became part of Regency architecture, continuing the style established in eighteenth century Bath. From the middle of the century terraces stretched the length of the kingdom to help house the growing population. From being an elegant form of town housing they became essential in providing houses for the lower middle classes and better paid artisans. By the end of the century the terrace house was a working class home; one whose rent was affordable and whose building standards were regulated by law.

In the Island we have examples of terraces built in the early nineteenth century, those designed for the middle classes, for industrial workers, as well as those built in seaside towns once the railways came in the 1860s. All these houses, whatever their social status, have similar features; all share a common facade, all share party walls, and all have narrow frontages. In the early years of the century the repeated pattern of terrace frontages was given interest with balconies, but later terraces repeated a standard form of house to whatever length was needed. Terraces built to rent grew gradually, they were speculative and the builder had to be sure of his return on the first houses within a terrace before he could add to it. But the demand for houses was persistent, and became overwhelming as the century advanced.

Lind Street, Ryde, includes St James's Terrace, completed about 1836. Standing on the south side it is a good illustration of modest building at this time. The line of the terrace is now broken by the Town Hall Chambers, built in 1853-54 as the Assembly Rooms, but the frontage shows how the gentle indentation of individual houses from their neighbours breaks up what could have been a monotonous line. The earliest houses, those to the east of the Assembly Rooms, each had a round-headed door entrance with a larger round-headed window on the ground floor. A linking feature throughout the terrace were the balconies outside the upper floor drawing room windows, delicate wrought iron in the earlier houses, replaced by more florid work in the west end houses, where larger windows indicate a changing style later in the century.

At the top of the social scale in Ryde was a grand terrace of ten houses built by the Player family between 1826-1829. Their architect, James Sanderson, planned a handsome block on a sloping site off St Thomas's Street, intended to be part of a larger scheme, a town square, but this was never realized. The terrace, now Brigstocke Terrace, remains, beautifully restored. The entrance front, with a large open space for carriages, faced towards St Thomas's church. From here each house was entered over an individual covered bridge spanning a wide basement area. The most pleasing front of Sanderson's building faced the sea. Here there was no basement, the four floors rising directly

from the ground, and the full effect of the Italianate design was shown. Two corner towers with wide eaves enclose the terrace and the central section is flanked by similar tower-like forms. All the decoration comes from long runs of iron balconies with canopies on the second floor, where the reception rooms looked out to sea. At the corner towers the balconies and canopies were carried to the floor above, giving added definition to this visually important terrace. This was a speculative venture, the houses being let on short leases. The occupiers were among the grandest people in Ryde and it not surprising to find Elizabeth, Countess of Clare, the benefactress of St Mary's Roman Catholic Church in Ryde, among the later residents.

Wrought iron balconies and canopies were common features in seaside terraces. Cowes has only a remnant of such a sea front terrace, now overwhelmed by Osborne Court, but at East Cowes, Cambridge Terrace remains. This attractive row of small houses, built during the 1870s in a style fashionable fifty or more years earlier, used iron decoration in much the same way as did Regency builders. It did not attract

Brigstocke Terrace, Ryde. This grand terrace was built by the Player family between 1826-29. Their architect, James Sanderson, designed ten houses for lease in an attractive Italianate style, reserving his main decoration for the front facing seaward, using iron balconies with canopies as the main feature. The tenants were families of means, including Elizabeth, Countess of Clare, the benefactress of the Roman Catholic church in Ryde.

Cambridge Terrace, East Cowes. This attractive row of houses was built in the 1870s but the style was that of an early Victorian seaside terrace.

the middle classes but was within reach of the top tier of working class families. Early tenants included two boat builders, a joiner and undertaker, a blockmaker and two widows who took in lodgers.

Taking in lodgers and visitors has been part of Island life since the opening of the nineteenth century. In most places they were welcomed, but not in cottages and houses in and near Ventnor where Lord Yarborough's tenants were prevented from adding to their income in this way. There were few houses suitable for summer visitors; in 1829 only about six furnished houses were suitable for 'gentlemen' to hire. Some invalids were already spending the winter in Ventnor and Bonchurch, but its gentle climate was not widely known until the 1840s when patients with chest complaints were recommended to spend the winter months in this 'Madeira' of the south coast.

The landscape of natural terraces filled with houses as the population doubled in ten years. Land was sold piecemeal by a bankrupt lord of the manor to small builders. 'The land has been let in small portions to needy people who have run up small houses for sale for the sake of immediate gain', wrote a visiting lady in March 1841. The average price for lodgings was two guineas a week for a sitting room, three bedrooms and the use of the kitchen but it rose to three guineas in July.

St Boniface Terrace was built during the 1840s just below St Boniface Down. Four pairs of large semi-detached houses, each with a basement and three upper floors, were built to accommodate visitors, as the 1851 census return for Ventnor shows. Number eight, was entered as a lodging house, the home of Alfred Lake, a twenty-five year old carpenter, his wife who ran the boarding house, their infant daughter and a sixteen year old maid. Three families lodged with them, an adult brother and sister and two widows, each with adult daughters. Four servants were also registered, probably employed by the paying guests. Altogether fifteen people lived in the house.

In 1866 the railway station opened, itself an additional attraction to the area under the down. St Boniface Terrace was conveniently close and by 1900 fifteen more houses were built. Much nearer the sea Dudley Terrace, Devonshire Terrace and Alexandra Terrace attracted middle class visitors, but as at East Cowes the houses of the poor were all too visible. Small houses built in St Catherine's Street, Cow Leas and Albert Street were 'squalid dwellings' that hurt middle class sensibilities.

Building a terrace was an uncertain prospect and expectations were not always realized. The history of Rosehill Terrace, now part of Drake Road, Newport, illustrates how risky such a speculation could be. In the 1850s the area around St John's church was being developed, with a middle class terrace in Bignor Place already established. In 1854 a piece of land was leased by Queen's College, Oxford, to Charles Saunders, a shipwright who lived at Porchfield. The lease ran for 1000 years and, as was usual at the time, Saunders paid an annual rent of £6.25 until building began. The following year he was joined by Albert William Beetham of Rosehill, Hampshire, probably as a mortgagee, and it was Beetham who regulated the form of development.

The intention clearly was to attract the type of middle class residents who were living nearby and there was provision for coach houses and stables to be built on the extreme western boundary, out of sight of neighbours. But the immediate hopes for this project came to nothing and it was only in 1881 that work on a small terrace began. The five yellow brick houses with red brick banding, full height bays and pretty dormer gables were substantial and attractive, but they were not easy to let. Ten years later only two were occupied, but these

The Mall, Newport. Alexandra Terrace was a major new development begun in 1863. It is a true Mall, with a wide area before the houses to create a promenade. The houses are brick and stucco, drawing much on Cubitt's work at Osborne, and the terrace is closed at each end with a double fronted house. This view was taken in 1938 when there was little traffic on the road.

tenants were representative of a new class of men who could afford to live in middle class surroundings. John Way was an engineer-millwright who had his son-in-law, another engineer, and an apprentice living with him. Next door was William George, a leather dresser. Both men had businesses in Newport and were the forerunners of other business men who were to live in this short terrace.

On the western boundary of Newport, at the beginning of Carisbrooke Road, a major development began in 1863 when the first bricks were laid on what was to be Alexandra Terrace, celebrating the new Princess

Alexandra. Visually this long handsome terrace is unique in the Island in having a wide frontage, which was raised up and railed off from the road, creating The Mall, a fashionable promenade where pedestrians could walk in safety well away from horses, carriages and wagons. The terrace was built in brick and stucco with a rusticated ground floor, a first floor with alternating balconies and bay windows and a top floor beneath deep eaves. A double-fronted house closed it at each end.

The space inside each house was restricted, with a narrow hall leading to the stairs, two ground floor rooms, one behind the other and an extension for the kitchen. The drawing room on the first floor took up the whole frontage, with two other rooms on this floor and further bedrooms under the eaves. There was only space for a small yard behind, linked to a back service lane for tradesmen.

Although externally grand, its early occupants were modest middle class families

with a significant number of widows and elderly spinsters living off dividends, rents and annuities, sufficient to allow them to keep one servant. In 1881 the census included the Wesleyan minister and his next door neighbour, the Primitive Methodist minister, neither of whom could have afforded high rents. Two businessmen appear, William Palmer, a miller's manager, and George Snelgrove, a house decorator whose niece, his assistant painter, lived with the family.

While the builder of Alexandra Terrace had created a fine facade, across the road another terrace was being built in a less ostentatious style but with the advantage of gardens behind. In 1862 three houses were built and the row gradually extended back towards Newport. The interior of one of the first houses to be built still retains much of the mid-Victorian style of this period. Built on a corner site, the house is entered by a small hall, separated by an archway from a larger hall with space for a

Alfred Street, East Cowes, is an example of early Victorian building for the working classes. Yellow brick houses were built each side of a narrow road. They retain an almost Regency simplicity with round-headed doors, outlined in red brick, as are the windows. Tall chimneys indicate the importance of coal fires to these families despite the high cost of fuel.

good staircase. The front room has a marble fireplace and behind it a room with French doors leading into the garden. Across the passage, behind the stairs, the small kitchen has a scullery off it and another small room tucked behind the kitchen. The first floor drawing room also has a marble fireplace and could be extended by opening wide double doors into a small room beside it. Four good bedrooms complete a comfortable middle class home with room to accommodate one or two servants.

Victorian semi-detached houses built in urban or suburban situations often resembled a

74

terrace, with only a narrow gap between each pair, and the internal arrangements remained those of a terrace house. Externally the builder would sometimes emphasize the shared nature of the houses by tiling the path before the two front doors in a single pattern. Repetition of decorative features also had a unifying effect. The builder could buy his various motifs in bulk and repeat them regularly on each house. The effect was to create rows of semi-detached houses which were, in all other respects, terraces.

The nature of Island life meant that the working class terraces of the northern industrial towns are not a major feature of our domestic buildings, but good examples can be found in East Cowes, where the shipbuilding yards offered full employment. Alfred Street, a narrow road rising from Clarence Road to Adelaide Grove, still shows the standard of housing adequate for the 1850s. Brick built, two up, two down, with a front door opening directly into a front room lighted by a single sash window, these small houses climb up the hill, unassuming but practical. At the end of the nineteenth century they were homes to a variety of workers, some directly connected with the sea – mariners, fishermen, shipwrights, riveters – while other occupants were general labourers, carpenters, plasterers and gardeners.

Speculative builders had no money to spare on decoration when Alfred Street was built, but as the century advanced mass production made better quality finishes possible for even small houses. Sometimes the builder achieved surprising results within the margin he could afford. In the opening years of the twentieth century Grange Road and St David's Road in East Cowes were being developed with short terraces of houses. This was a time when the town was growing rapidly. A sale catalogue published in 1909 spoke of the area as 'ripe for building of small class houses . . . for which

A terrace house in Grange Road, East Cowes. This was part of the development of East Cowes at the opening of the twentieth century. Built in red brick with yellow brick facings the upper windows transform these houses. The double arches look back to Norris Castle and Osborne, but economy dictated false arches fitted to rectangular windows for the sashes.

there is a steady demand'. The houses in these roads met that demand. Built in red brick with yellow facings, the ground floors have conventional brick bays beside the front door, but the upper windows transform the rows. Each house has a window framed by a double arch in yellow brick, the two lights separated by an iron column, fluted in the lower section, with a suggestion of acanthus leaves in the apex decoration. The sash windows follow the curve of the arch, and it is only when the windows are open that we see that the straight rectangles of glass have false arches fitted over them. The long shadow of Norris Castle and Osborne, with their round-headed windows, still continued to influence housing at the end of the century, whilst mass production allowed working people to enjoy features once reserved only for the upper classes. Inside, while cheap match-boarding was used for the staircase

walls, the front bedroom with its double light window had a fireplace decorated with glazed tiles of tall Art Nouveau tulips.

The most distinctive street of workers' houses is found in Newport where Caesars Road remains an unaltered example of housing more typical of the north of England. They were built in the late nineteenth century, the whole street being gradually extended on both sides, the general style remaining the same, but minor variations showing where new building began. All the houses are red brick with yellow brick facings and are unadorned. Some have the front door set back in a small porch, the doors of others are in line with the facade. Inside, a narrow passage leads to the back living room, which is separated from the front room by a steep staircase. The living room at the back was lit by a window looking into the garden. An annexe at one side provided a scullery where the sink, boiler, and, in the twentieth century, the oil cooker were housed. The lavatory was built against the garden wall

Caesars Road, Newport. This exceptional street of workers' houses, reminiscent of northern England, was built in stages from the end of the nineteenth century. Round-headed doors continued to be used, but fashionable red brick was used throughout. The growth of the terrace can be seen by minor changes in the brickwork, as can be seen here, but the overall effect was unchanged from beginning to end.

which separated each of these narrow properties from its neighbour.

By the time these houses were built there were regulations governing new building, including by-laws which set standards for window size, height of rooms and space at the rear of each house. The width of streets was also determined and a comparison of narrow Alfred Street with Caesars Road and Grange Road shows how state regulation, even when it was permissive, improved living conditions by the end of Queen Victoria's reign. The way houses functioned as family units shows the continuing influence of Victorian social standards. However small the space it had to be divided into several compartments, just as larger houses were. Rooms for particular purposes were as valued in these small terrace houses as they were in the larger terrace houses on the Mall. The front room has often been derided by later generations, but in social terms it was an important public room, performing the same function as a middle class drawing room, a place to receive guests, to celebrate family events, to show off the best furniture and ornaments. It was the most obvious declaration that working class people were aspiring to middle class standards.

NINE

The Comfortable Home

A visitor to Totland Bay in the 1890s described the 'handsome residences' that were being built there, 'that very latest thing in Victorian architecture; all turrets and gables and balconies and red brick and white paint.' In this summary of the developing seaside resort we have the essence of the change in house style which reached its distinctive form in the years before the First World War.

The source of this new style lay in the much grander country houses being built for the new rich in the last quarter of the nineteenth century. The long agricultural depression reduced the value of land, leaving those whose security depended on farm rents in a precarious situation. By contrast, manufacturing and business were booming. Fortunes could be made within a generation. The newly rich could afford to build large, rambling houses which displayed to the world the wealth that lay behind them. They might not be able to claim by descent the lineage of old landed families, but their houses could be built in such

Foreland House, Bembridge. This large turreted house is an example of houses built before the First World War, often as seaside homes for wealthy families. The windows, with small panes of glass in the upper lights are typical of this period.

In 1870 the Totland Bay Estate Company planned 'a new watering place'. They chose an empty landscape and built the essential pier. In 1880 the grand Totland Bay Hotel was built on a prominent site not far from the pier and from this time the new village of Totland grew. The first of the large Edwardian houses can be seen in this view. The hotel has gone, replaced by Amman Court, named after a former owner of the hotel, but many of the seaside homes remain, with their turrets and black and white beams. These with the smaller village houses still make Totland an Edwardian enclave.

a way that they appeared to have grown over the centuries, rather than as the sudden result of trade and industry. Medieval towers, jettied upper floors, oriel windows and Tudor gables all became fashionable, as did the tile-hung gables and casement windows of the old vernacular houses of southern England.

New houses, which included many of these features, attracted an increasingly wealthy upper middle class. Soon they were being built in the countryside and on green fields at the edge of towns. There was space for them to spread horizontally, and there were still

sufficient servants for the largest to include considerable room for domestic offices well separated from the family. In the Isle of Wight it was sea views that attracted prospective house purchasers or tenants. But much depended on where they were. Gurnard was intended to develop as a garden village built on land belonging to James Wilkinson of Shalfleet. He died in 1850 with no direct descendants and the estate was divided into large building plots. These were sold piecemeal with no overall direction and the land was slow in being developed. The first plot was bought by the Pritchett family of brickmakers who set up a brickyard nearby and by the end of the century some large houses were built along the main avenue, Worsley Road. But this development was no more successful than that at East Cowes in the early years of the century.

Totland, however, had better prospects. In 1870 the Totland Bay Estate Company was formed with definite plans to create 'a new watering place'. There was space to build a pier and a handsome hotel. Large holiday homes in spacious grounds appeared. A new village of terrace houses and shops grew up, the frontages covered in pebbledash and mock Tudor beams. By the turn of the century Totland was a lively summer resort. But its heyday was shortlived, the First World War intervened and the resort never regained its original elegance and style. Some of the large houses remain, still with their turrets and gables, monuments to wealth which built and sustained them.

Freshwater Bay was also being built up. Edward Lear, visiting the Tennysons in 1864, saw this 'quiet part of the Island fast spoiling' with plans for a new road, hundreds of houses and a proposed railway. His anxiety was premature, although the houses did appear once the railway to Freshwater opened to passengers in 1880. From this time the village centre was built up, situated at a point between the old settlement near the church and Freshwater Bay. It still retains much of the character of the Edwardian period, as does the Avenue, whose detached houses link Edwardian Freshwater with Edwardian Totland.

New building in the west of the Island was on open land with wide vistas. Edwardian growth on the eastern shores of the Island was much more dominant. The little fishing village of Seaview erupted with new building. Rows of bay-windowed houses, with porches, verandas, balconies and much black and white woodwork were built facing the sea at Seagrove Bay. All this had been stimulated by the new Seaview Pier, which opened in 1881, giving the resort, for the first time, direct and easy connection to the mainland and ensuring a demand for summer holiday accommodation in this corner of the Island.

Around the point at Bembridge the arrival of the railway in 1882 had a similar impact. In the 1890s some splendid family houses were built in the High Street. Hidden behind high walls, their privacy was secured while the occupants enjoyed views down to the Haven. Decorative

Stephen Salter designed this group of cottages in Nettlestone. They show his skill in achieving a picturesque effect, even when he was working to a limited budget, and add considerably to the entrance of the village from Ryde.

Sydney Lodge, Ryde. This romantic house was designed in 1885 by Stephen Salter, probably the first house he built in the Island. Salter worked in Oxford and the Thames valley before moving to the Island and establishing a practice here. Sydney Lodge was built for Thomas Dodsworth of Blackheath, London, as a holiday home, the first of many well-built, attractive houses designed for the upper middle classes by Stephen Salter.

date stones, many roofs, tall chimneys and timber-decorated gables continue to distinguish them to this day. In Ducie Avenue, the tree-shaded approach to the village from the sea, stands Balure, in its spacious garden but still with less ground than originally surrounded the house. This was the home of Lady de Roebuck, Lady-in-Waiting to Queen Mary, who stayed with her when she was visiting Bembridge.

In a quiet lane at the edge of Ryde two handsome houses were built on sites which gave long seaward views over farmlands. They were designed by Stephen Salter, a local architect, for two brothers, both military men with substantial family wealth from shipping interests. Perivale House in Playstreet Lane was built for Major Edward Croft Murray, and Horsenden, now Rye House, for his brother Lieutenant Colonel Croft Murray. Unlike so many of these large Edwardian houses the original Horsenden remains a family home, standing in grounds whose shrubs and lawns retain their Edwardian character. The muted red brick, towers, many windows, crisp white paint, decorative black beams and pargetting, contain all the elements clients looked for from their architects. Stephen Salter more than met these requirements in this fine house.

The interior also satisfied current fashion, making the hall the centre of the building, with all the ground floor rooms opening off it. It was designed to carry a wide staircase rising through the whole height of the building, an illustration in itself of the lavish use of space – a distinguishing feature of these houses. Equally typical were the servants' quarters behind a firmly closed door at the back of the hall, with their own staircase and working area arranged so that they had no view of the family garden.

Some Island residents were rebuilding their houses to bring them up to date. At Nunwell Stephen Salter was employed to design an attractive lodge at the main entrance to the estate. In 1895 Nunwell House was extended when a new dining room was added to the garden wing. Finally, in the opening years of the twentieth century, the almost obligatory country house billiard room was added, opening into the garden and linked by a short of flight of steps to the dining room. The new room was designed by Percy Stone, the distinguished Island antiquarian and architect. It was built to a tight schedule. On the 10 May 1902 Stone asked John Henry Glynn Oglander to sign his estimate so that he could put work in hand. By the 28 July Stone was lamenting a decision by the family to open the room with a dance during Cowes week, thus putting pressure on the workmen. His suggestion of 'Turkey Red and white for the walls and ceiling in yellow and white' must have created a striking scene, if adopted, but, with help from the family, all was ready for the dance. Mrs Florence Oglander was content; she wrote in her diary, 'I was . . . wheeled through the door of the new room to watch the dancing . . . They danced hard until 3.30 and were very merry.'

Percy Stone wished to keep the exterior simple. In May he advised against a 'Dutch Gable' to hide the skylight as the wall was high enough and, 'I think a gable doing nothing is rather "false art"'. But the family did not agree, the gable was built. It stands today, demonstrating that Stone was right in his judgement. Despite this he was clearly proud of

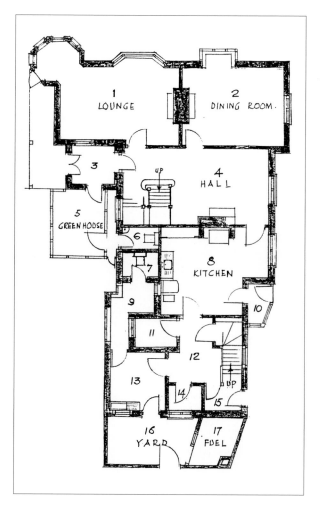

Ground floor plan of Long Close, Freshwater Bay. This house was built about 1898 on rising ground overlooking the marsh. The entrance hall at the centre of this plan was a hall-sitting room, an innovation adopted from Edwardian country houses. The following rooms, numbered on the plan, are: 3 - porch, 6 - family WC with entrance from the garden, 7 - servants' WC, 9 - lobby, 10 - tradesmen's entrance, 11 - pantry, 12 - lobby, 13 and 14 service rooms, 15 external door to back stairs and lobby. A detached laundry stood in an enclosed yard.

his contribution to the house. In 1909 he wrote to John Henry Oglander, 'I see from your letter that you intend me to keep the p.card. Many thanks as it is the only record I have of my small addition to Nunwell.'

At nearby Morton House, Brading, a thorough restoration was undertaken. A villa had stood on the site from the early nineteenth century, gradually acquiring additional rooms. When Mr John Fardell and his family came to Morton in 1903 the house was reconstructed and given a modern interior. The dining room remains a fine example of this period. The fireplace, decorated with William de Morgan tiles, includes a carved wooden text, 'East, West, Home's Best' – a pithy summary of both Victorian and Edwardian sentiments. Percy Stone may well have designed the room. John Fardell and he were brothers-in-law and he certainly designed a set of plain dining chairs for the house, a not unusual practice at the time when Arts and Crafts architects created furniture to fit the rooms they planned.

Another house which was considerably altered to suit the taste of the period was Billingham, between Chillerton and Chale, where a whole courtyard was enclosed to provide a new dining room and bedrooms. Similarly, in the 1890s a new house was built near the entrance gate to the manor, which unlike the manor's additions, still remains. Architecturally, it is a muddle of different influences. A stone porch with a room above has a seventeenth century source, the deeply hipped roof draws on the late seventeenth and early eighteenth century and the ground floor casements have their origins in the late eighteenth century. But combined with red brick and pebbledash it is an unmistakably Edwardian house.

New houses for the comfortable middle classes kept the same division between family rooms and servants' quarters as in large country houses; often the space allowed for the kitchen and offices equalled, or exceeded that for family rooms. Nothing is more telling than the elaborate subdivision of space for particular domestic household functions. A typical house in Afton Road, Freshwater, includes all the essential characteristics (see the plan on the opposite page). Set back from the road, secluded behind hedges and shrubs, 'Long Close' house stands on an elevated site with views over the marsh to the sea. The back garden was large enough to include a tennis court and kitchen garden. The hall was the centre of the house and was large enough to include a wide staircase near, but out of sight of, the front door, so that the visitor stepped into a welcoming hall with a fireplace, comfortable armchairs and convenient tables. Opening from it were the dining room and drawing room, both facing the front of the house. Light was an important element in these rooms. In the drawing room the base of the tower makes an alcove with windows in each of the five angles, adding to the light already entering the room from a deep bay window. Across the hall was the door to the kitchen. The tradesmen's entrance at the side of the house led into a small lobby just outside the kitchen, with convenient shelves on which deliveries could be left. The larder with its cold slate shelf was tucked under the back stairs; opposite was the pantry, with cupboards for china and glass. A separate scullery led directly off the kitchen. Other small rooms were for specific functions, now long since abandoned, boot and shoe cleaning, knife sharpening and silver polishing, whilst the laundry room stood at the back of an enclosed yard.

The most significant new room upstairs was the bathroom over the entrance porch, often the most convenient space available. Hot water was piped to it from a tank heated by the kitchen range. One bathroom for such a large house might seem inadequate, but it was not used by all the family. Washstands were still important items of bedroom furniture, and ladies continued to wash in their own bedrooms. All the pipes in bathrooms and lavatories were exposed so that they could be easily cleaned. The free-standing cast iron bath was sometimes set on a lead base to protect wooden floors, as was Princess Beatrice's bath

LEFT Duver House, overlooking St Helen's harbour, is another Stephen Salter house. Here he used Art Nouveau ideas for the upper windows, while at the back of the house a wall is decorated with a large pargetted sunflower.

in Carisbrooke Castle. Exposed, decorated lavatory bowls were more hygienic than the Victorian WCs encased in mahogany boxes, but the mahogany seat remained.

At about the same time a distinctive group of houses was being built on open farmland overlooking the sea at Bouldnor near Yarmouth. They are rare examples in the Island of large Edwardian 'bungalows'. Their situation, isolated and with direct access to the sea, and their design, low and wide with deep verandas and wide windows, emphasizes a new carefree open-air style of living, challenging the more formal standards of regular family life. These houses are not strictly bungalows as they have upper floor bedrooms, but their style was derived from Indian colonial bungalows with their deep verandas covered by a penthouse roof.

BELOW Kleffens, Bouldnor, Yarmouth, is one of four seaside bungalows built in 1897. Their inspiration was the Indian colonial bungalow with rooms sheltered by a veranda, but they also continue the English tradition of the picturesque cottage. The houses were not small, they could accommodate staff, and were the holiday homes of upper class families. Here the windows, door and veranda, with its turned wooden posts, are unaltered.

The four houses were built in 1897 and are typical holiday homes of well-to-do families. Externally they have the same features, tiled roofs, and tall chimneys, glazed ceramic tiles for the veranda and turned posts supporting the roof. A central door with glazed upper panels and bay windows on each side is all that can be seen of each house from the front, but this conceals a comfortable-sized house within. A long wide entrance hall floored with black and white geometric tiles had three rooms off it. The staircase was hidden at the back of the hall, beyond which was the bathroom, while kitchen and offices occupied the back of the house. Not all the houses used this basic layout in the same way. Cheriton dispensed with a door into the parlour. Instead a wide opening led directly from the hall, creating an informal

This view of the entrance hall at Swainston, Calbourne, in the early twentieth century shows exactly the informal, welcoming atmosphere of a hall-sitting room.

hall-sitting-room. Fretwork brackets, still in place, filled the upper corners of this entry, and more fretwork was used in an arch separating the hall from the stairs.

Ideas which were used in expensive homes filtered down to smaller builders and were adapted to suit the pockets of ordinary working people. One of the most significant trends in the last years of Queen Victoria's reign was the general fall in prices, while wage levels remained stationary or rose. In half a century many workers moved into the lower levels of the middle classes and could consider living in a modern house. For them a semi-detached house, pebbledashed, with a gable decorated with wood framing and a sheltered porch was a dream home. The front room with its bay and the back dining/living room with French windows into the garden had Art Nouveau door knobs, finger plates and keyhole covers in copper bronze finish. All these were included in a semi-detached house at Lake, where careful planning allowed for a small raised sitting area off the hall with a window and space for one or two chairs and a table. The idea of the hall/sitting room had been achieved.

These Edwardian houses are a significant part of our domestic history, introducing the modern house, but they were built for only a short period from the 1890s to the outbreak of the First World War. Compared with our modern stock of houses they are few in number and those that remain, whether large or small, are important examples of domestic architecture at a moment that neatly defines the end of an era.

ABOVE The hall of a small Edwardian house at Lake, Sandown. The architect has contrived an area off the stairs large enough for a table and one or two chairs, in fact, a hall-sitting room.

BELOW An Art Nouveau fingerplate in copper, typical of door furnishings in Edwardian Houses.

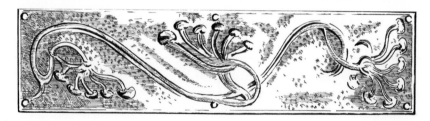

TEN

Arts and Crafts Houses – Return to the Vernacular

While Victorian England was indulging in Gothic or classical building, a quiet revolution was taking place in some architects' practices. Signs of this were already present in the 1840s when architects such as George Street and William Butterfield were building houses that, although still Gothic, were relatively simple, with steep gable roofs, tall chimneys and porches. By this time there was already an understanding that the old vernacular farmhouses, fitting so naturally into the countryside, were valuable sources for domestic architecture. From the drawing office of George Street there emerged two men, Philip Webb and Norman Shaw, who were to use the vernacular in a way that still influences house design.

William Morris, the chief advocate of the nineteenth-century Arts and Craft movement, and Philip Webb, Street's chief assistant, were responsible for building a house, completed in 1860, which led the way into what is now called the Domestic Revival. The Red House, Bexley Heath, was built for Morris at the time of his marriage. It was a large, even grand house, but it was built of plain red brick, with windows placed to meet the needs of the rooms and spaces within the house and not to create an external effect. The steep tiled roof, tall chimney stacks, porthole windows and simple brick Gothic arches used over the doors and windows were to be taken up by many later architects and builders. Marvel Lodge, a small house just outside Newport, is a miniature Red

House. Built during the 1870s in red brick, an L-shaped building with a small turret joining the two wings, it includes porthole windows and above the windows facing the road Gothic brick arches are defined, adapting Philip Webb's ideas to what was a modest new farmhouse.

The widespread use of Arts and Crafts ideas had to wait until the twentieth century and in the Island we do have buildings that are closely associated with the movement. Bembridge School, particularly, through its founder, J. Howard Whitehouse, and his architect M.H. Baillie Scott, has firm foundations in the tradition. Howard Whitehouse had been involved in social work at Bournville, Cadbury's model village near Birmingham, before he founded Bembridge School in 1919 and his ideas for the new school buildings were drawn from the vernacular style of workers' houses he had seen there. Indeed, he chose W. A. Harvey, the major architect at Bournville, to work with him in designing the external form of the school chapel.

M.H. Baillie Scott was a significant architect in the Arts and Crafts tradition. He and Whitehouse had met in 1914 when they were both involved in improving housing for Scottish miners. It was natural that the founder of a school which was to base its education on the ideas of the Arts and Crafts movement should choose an architect who was deeply rooted in the tradition. By 1927 Baillie Scott had completed a group of buildings

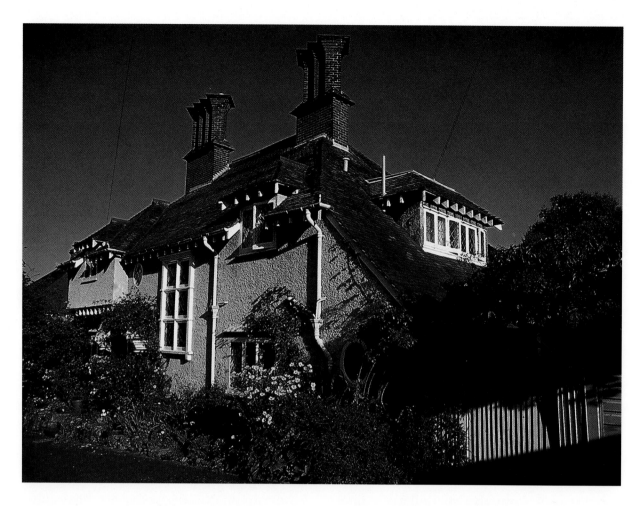

overlooking the garden, including the Warden's House and a set of rooms with dormitories over them. They were brick-built in the vernacular style with a deep tile-hung roof, wide eaves and strong chimney stacks. These, with the casement windows and plank doors, show how important the influence of the old farmhouse tradition was to Arts and Crafts architects. An extension was added to the Warden's House in 1929 to provide a large ground floor room and an upper room in which Whitehouse's collection of drawings, paintings and literary works of John Ruskin could be displayed. These rooms, with their planked floors and wide windows, still evoke the charm of the William Morris tradition.

The style evolved in a rather different manner in the drawing office of Norman Shaw. His

Magnolia House, Newport, designed in 1924 for a veterinary surgeon by Stephen Salter in the latter part of his career. This house shows the influence of the Arts and Crafts movement on his work; tall chimneys with oversailing tops, irregularly placed windows to fit the rooms within the house and the large window, which is filled with coloured glass, to light the stairs. When it was first built the exterior pebbledash was unpainted and the whole house would have been much more sombre.

houses also drew on southern counties farmhouses and urban domestic buildings, but he created distinctive buildings which came into general fashion when suburban houses began to fill green fields in the years following the First World War. A good example of how the style was used locally can be seen in Cypress Road, Newport. This house was designed by Stephen Salter in 1924 for J. Cowper-Blake, a veterinary surgeon with a wide practice, who could afford to build in the best modern style. Cowper-Blake, his wife and sister lived here with a single resident maid, showing clearly the change in domestic staffing following the 1914-18 war. Indoor servants were at a premium and daily women came in to help with the housework. The garden was staffed by a full-time gardener and one working part-time, but this was a household of dedicated gardeners who created an Italianate paved garden as the central feature of the view from their drawing room window.

The two sets of tall chimneys with oversailing tops immediately attract the eye, while the wood-planked and coved canopy over the door is typical Shaw. A long rectangular window lights the stairs and the irregular casements show how the placing of the interior rooms determined the external appearance of the house. The frontage of the building is today painted cream, but in 1924 the pebbledash was un-painted, a reminder that our present love of light colours distorts the intentions of the earlier architects. Exposed beams at the eaves, and supporting a jettied upper room, all contribute to the vernacular spirit and on the garden front a gabled bay includes tile hanging and many lights in the bay window.

Indoors the Arts and Crafts tradition prevails, with exposed rafters, painted black, planked doors hung on long iron hinges and planked built-in cupboards, originally painted black. The fireplaces in the ground floor rooms are red brick, with simple arch openings, flush to the wall, with plain wood mantel shelves above. The largest room is the long drawing room, with its low ceiling and exposed rafters, where the deep bay window and French windows look down on the garden. Both the study/surgery and dining room were modest in size, as was the kitchen, placed right beside the dining room. Nothing demonstrated more the

M.H. Baillie Scott's illustration of one of his cottages built in St Lawrence in 1936. Baillie Scott was a noted Arts and Crafts architect whose cottages were particularly admired. It was included in a pamphlet he wrote at this time explaining his principle that traditional style could be combined with labour-saving features within the house.

change in domestic arrangements following the war than the siting of the kitchen; servants could not be put at a distance from the family, there were too few of them, and practical convenience had to be built into house design. The maid's bedroom was a comfortably sized room on the same floor as the family, though it remained the only bedroom without a corner wash basin.

This house has been described in some detail as it includes features used in all Arts and Crafts houses, although the style in which they were built varied. Baillie Scott was particularly noted for his cottages. He was described in 1905 as 'a poet' in whose houses 'every single room, down to the smallest detail is thought out as a place to be lived in'. Certainly in the three cottages he designed for a site in St Lawrence his romantic spirit produced what appear to be old houses, although they were built in 1937.

In a booklet produced to promote the development he summed up his convictions. The house 'must be sincere and true . . . a genuine expression of our practical requirements and human needs.' His houses were designed from within outwards, the thatched roofs, dormer windows, latched casement windows and nail-studded doors drawing on traditional sources, while the interior was designed for the 1930s housewife who did her own work, with help from a daily woman.

The external appearance of the three cottages is similar but each has an individual interior. St Anne's standing high above the road has one long, well-proportioned sitting room on one side of the front door. St Lawrence is a much larger house than its cottage front would suggest. A wide staircase rises from a hall with a sitting room and dining room on each side. In this house both rooms have small square hatch doors connecting with the service rooms, the dining room opening into the pantry and the sitting room hatch opening into a series of built-in cupboards. Upstairs a long corridor serves two bedrooms at the front of the house and a bathroom at the extreme end. In one bedroom a walk-in wardrobe remains, as does the hand basin; a small corner wash basin in the back bedroom is also part of the original fittings. In the house, as in the other two, cupboards were fitted into convenient spaces in rooms and passages.

Farthings, the third cottage, is much more of a cottage, with stairs rising directly from the front door. The sitting room is exceptionally well lit with windows in each external wall. In the dining room a large inglenook fireplace takes up most of one wall. Built in brick, it included a bread oven and a bench built into one side. These make-believe modern cottages were not cheap, one was sold for about £1,250 in 1937, but they did attract middle class families who were looking for a seaside home.

Meanwhile, a movement to protect old
domestic buildings saw the restoration of old
farmhouses and cottages by enthusiasts with
money to spend. Its origins lay in the Society
for Protecting Ancient Buildings, founded by
William Morris in 1877, but it was in the inter-
war years that rescue work on farmhouses and
cottages began in the Island. The major
restoration was that of Mottistone Manor, then
an old neglected farmhouse on the Seely estate.
In 1925-26 General Jack Seely decided to leave
Brook House and live at Mottistone, entrusting
to his son John, a young architect, and his
partner Paul Paget, the task of bringing the old
house back to life. It was a major undertaking
for two young architects and General Seely
took the precaution of having their plans
viewed by Edward Lutyens before the work
began. It was no easy task to remove the earth
bank which had slipped onto the back of the
house, and the interior work of making a
sixteenth-century house suitable for twentieth-
century occupation needed both skill and care.

By 1928 the work was completed and an
article in *Country Life* of that year approved
their success: 'They have respected, and, where
necessary, restored the old work, but have met
modern requirements with imagination and
economy. It was not easy to do as much as has
been done here . . . without its appearing either
over-restored, or interesting but uncomfort-
able. Mottistone strikes the happy medium . . .
The past is one with the present.'

Ten years later a much smaller but still
significant restoration was undertaken at
Chale. Downend Cottage was in a derelict state
in 1938 when it was bought by Captain and
Mrs Horsley to give themselves a home within
sight and sound of the sea. The original
features of the seventeenth century farmhouse
were revealed, including beams with heart-
shaped stoppings and large open fireplaces.
One included a bread oven at one side which
they illuminated with a small electric light to
show off the brickwork, a device familiar to
present day restorers. The finished building,
with the inevitably added porch, was a plain
unadorned cottage with a thatched roof.

A second cottage, Goodalls, which had been
condemned for human habitation, was also
rescued by the Horsleys and here, too, beams
and fireplaces were saved. Both these houses
lent themselves to restoration in the Arts and
Crafts style, and they retain cupboards and
doors typical of the period.

The style of the vernacular farmhouse was adapted in the years between the wars as architects followed the model of C. E. A. Voysey, whose long, low-built country houses, with their sweeping roofs, horizontal windows and stone or brick walls continued the Arts and Crafts tradition. Local architects who worked to these standards designed houses that are now recognized as historic examples of their time. In the Island a number of such houses were built on the main road between Newport and Ryde, near Quarr Abbey. Set behind deep front gardens with lawns and flower borders, these houses with their leaded windows and Tudor-style porches speak as much of the pleasant lives enjoyed by the middle classes of the pre-Second World War period as do the black and white beamed houses of the Edwardian summer before the First World War. They were built for well-to-do professional people and the study of one house will indicate features of many others.

The Warren, Elenor's Grove, was built for Mr H. E. Jarvis, a local solicitor, by Gordon Sinden, an architect builder who had already built similar houses in this area in the 1930s. His speculative houses sold at about one thousand pounds but The Warren was built to order and included a detached billiard room, undoubtedly increasing the cost. Built in brick, with tile hanging, tall chimneys and a stone porch it was typical the Sussex farmhouse style of these Quarr houses. The long entrance hall with a purely decorative fireplace hints at the Edwardian hall-sitting room but the main room now was the lounge, a large room which ran from the front to the back of the house. Here were collected all the features of an old farmhouse, a solid wood oak door with iron handle, low ceiling, a wood floor and a large inglenook fireplace built from old stone blocks supporting a heavy oak beam. A smaller dining room with a brick fireplace overlooked the entrance drive and across the hall was the kitchen facing onto the back garden. A narrow passage led to a planked back door and off this, near the kitchen, was the scullery with its sink and next to it a walk-in larder with shelves of cool white tiles, much used at this time for kitchens, bathrooms and lavatories. An oak staircase with seventeenth-century style balusters led to a wide landing and five bedrooms. In two of these rooms deep walk-in wardrobes were the size of small rooms, giving ample storage space. A bathroom and lavatory completed the upper floor. This household, with sons living away from home, employed no resident staff but relied on daily help in the house and garden.

One architect of distinction who has left an example of his work in the Island is Oliver Hill, a man with original and idiosyncratic ideas about houses. He was greatly impressed by Lutyens and the tradition of using good materials, but he also enthusiastically absorbed the ideas of modern European architects in the inter-war years. For private clients he could produce a house to meet their needs, whether these were traditional or modern, and in 1928 he built a seaside home for Maxwell and Margaret Garnett, at Seaview. The house has sweeping gables, a tiled roof, plain metal windows and wooden shutters and large porthole windows. This was a family holiday home designed to be 'labour saving', even the skirtings being curved to avoid dust traps. It was an amalgam of traditional and modern, and its success was celebrated by the Garnetts with an engraved window including their own names, that of the architect, and a list of all the workers, including the lowliest apprentice.

Oliver Hill managed to combine the two architectural legacies drawn from the Arts and Crafts movement. In England it continued in the form of traditional housing, but in Europe the ideas of the movement were developed in much more radical ways, always retaining the principle that the form of a building should

In 1928 this unusual house was built in Seaview as a holiday home for the Garnett family. The architect was Oliver Hill, a successful and versatile architect whose working life was mainly between the wars. The sweeping roof with its green tiles is an example of Hill's delight in using colour in architecture.

follow its function and that materials should be suitable to their use. Modern materials in the inter-war years were steel and concrete. The result was houses that were cuboid in shape, concrete built, with flat roofs and wide metal windows. The first such houses appeared in Britain in 1925, but few were built before the outbreak of war. At seaside resorts the style was used for hotels and public buildings and at Cowes one dominant block remains to illustrate the style.

Osborne Court, an unmistakable part of the Parade, was built in 1938. It was a speculative development of flats undertaken by the Central London Property Trust, designed by Richard Jones, who was at the same time working on large buildings on the Sussex coast. At Cowes he faced some tricky problems, as the development had to be fitted into a small space and still ensure that most flats had a sea view. Timing was not on his side. The first occupants arrived in April 1939 and by September war had begun. Many of the flats were requisitioned for naval personnel and in 1942 the whole building became HMS *Vectis*. The real life of Osborne Court only began in 1945 when it was already out of date as an architectural feature.

Osborne Court, Cowes, a late example of modern design, built in 1938 by the London Property Trust. The steel and concrete structure, covered in 'Snowcrete', housed fifty two labour-saving service flats. From 1942 the building became H.M.S *Vectis* and it was only in 1945 that it began its real life as a domestic building.

In order to build the fifty-two flats which occupied six floors a terrace of early nineteenth century houses was demolished. The building which replaced them met all the requirements of a block of luxury flats, with communal services, a resident house manager and an indoor swimming pool. The structure was typical of the modern movement, a steel frame with reinforced concrete roof, walls, floors and stairs, and Crittall metal windows. The architect used the narrow space skilfully, stepping back the U-shaped form with curved balconies, so that it had something of the appearance of a cruise liner, shining white with 'Snowcrete' and looking out to sea. Above the entrance door sailing boats were etched in the glass, reflecting the real boats darting about the harbour.

Tenants were provided with central heating and hot water from a coke boiler, their garbage was removed through shutes to the ground floor and tradesmen delivered their goods by dumb waiter to each flat. They were comfortable and convenient small homes, some with one bedroom, others with two. In 1980 Number 33 was still much as it had been forty two years earlier, with a square entrance hall off which were the kitchen, bathroom and living room. The kitchen walls were covered to two thirds height with large cream tiles, finished with a narrow black rim and a final row of tiles. A fitted unit along one wall included a drop-down enamel working surface, a fitted broom cupboard and the garbage cupboard connecting with the shute. The original kitchen also included a refrigerator. The living room, opening onto a small balcony, included a single built-in fitment of shelves and cupboards which incorporated an electric fire, wireless loud speaker and an electric clock, a very compact use of space. One of the disadvantages of fitting so many flats into a small area and providing as many sea views as possible was that both bedrooms were entered directly from the living room and were separate from the bathroom. The balcony, too, while it provided a sea view, was overlooked by neighbours, as were most of the flats. A third flaw, which could not be overcome, was the shadow of the southern wing, which lay over some of the balconies most of the day.

Osborne Court was an intrusion into the small genteel houses on Cowes sea front and yet it gave a dramatic quality to the town as one approached from the sea. Its style is shared by a single house in Ward Avenue, Cowes, and we should be grateful that examples of a short-lived domestic style remain for us to see. The Osborne Court style was never very popular, although ideas from the modern movement were adapted to suburban homes and absorbed into the older traditional forms of which the British are so fond.

The entrance hall, Osborne Court.

ELEVEN

The Suburban House – a Private Castle

Between 1919 and 1939 nearly four million houses were built in England and Wales. It was a remarkable achievement and went far to solve the housing problems which had plagued the nineteenth century. The majority of these houses were built privately and were bought by the growing middle classes who, for the first time in large numbers, could afford houses of their own. The inflationary period following immediately on the end of the First World War gave place in the late 1920s and 1930s to a period of low interest rates and low material costs for building. At the same time men who had secure work with guaranteed, although often modest wages, could anticipate buying a home through a building society. These societies had been established since the 1830s, the Ryde and East Medina Society was founded in 1867, but they were both local and small scale.

The big expansion in house buying came with the growth of the national building societies in the late twenties and thirties. Building societies in the 1930s would accept members with a salary or wage of about four pounds a week. Deposits of 5% on the valuation of a property and repayment periods of twenty-five to thirty years for a weekly payment of between 75p and £1.50 made a new house possible. Bank employees, civil servants, lower paid professionals and some teachers might well afford a house at £1,000. Skilled craftsmen could consider lower priced houses, though the initial deposit was a problem. This was

overcome in the 1930s when a special fund was established which lent the deposit to the prospective buyer's building society and it became part of the long term repayment. Local authorities were also prepared to make long term loans at low interest.

What were these new owners looking for? In 1874 the newly incorporated Vectis Permanent Building Society encapsulated the dream of home-owners in their seal; a round Tudor-like

The seal of the Vectis Building Society. Permanent Building Societies began to develop in the 1840s, but the 1874 Building Societies Act gave them more security as they became limited companies with a legal status. This would have influenced the Vectis Building Society which was founded that year. The seal shows a castle with domestic chimneys and windows, a confirmation that the Englishman's home was his castle.

The Vicarage, Lake, was designed in 1930 by E L. Smith, a Newport architect. The sober brick house was left unadorned, except for a modified Gothic arch over the door, the traditional indication that this was a clergy house. It is a good example of the Arts and Crafts tradition interpreted by a local architect, using a traditional material with modern Crittall windows.

castle, topped with domestic windows and chimneys. The Englishman's home was his castle, and twentieth century families looked for the same security and privacy which had previously been possible only for those with substantial means. Rented accommodation could not bring that sense of well-being which came when the front door closed on a personal piece of property.

We are so used to seeing houses of this period that one might think they had appeared fully fledged at Ideal Home Exhibitions and in the many books local builders could draw on for plans, costings and interior fittings. But in each

suburban house there was the influence of the Edwardian Arts and Crafts architects. E.L. Smith, a Newport architect working at this time, shows in his work how the ideas of Edwardian times were adapted to the post-war period. The Church of England, in its historic tradition of building parsonages in the current best style, chose Smith to design the new vicarage of the Church of the Good Shepherd, Lake, in 1930. He produced a house which combined elements of the Edwardian style with the most up-to-date features of the time. Edwardian spaciousness was established in the drive, which swept round from one wide entrance gate to another; its ecclesiastical association identified by the brick Gothic arch framing the front door.

The spacious hall with its wood block floor, panelling, and wide staircase created a sombre entrance, but both the drawing room and dining room were flooded with light from the square leaded lights of the Crittall windows. In

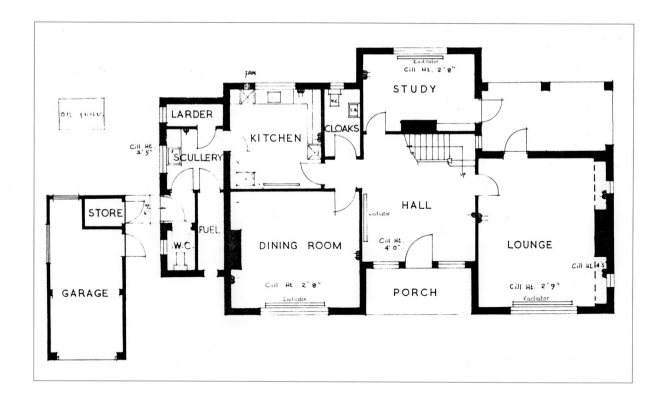

Ground floor plan of Lake Vicarage. The large lounge (drawing room) and dining room reflect the use of the vicarage as a meeting place for church members. The drawing room and study opened onto a veranda supported by pillars.

the drawing room additional light came from long narrow windows in Arts and Crafts style set each side of the fireplace. Both fireplaces retain dark wood surrounds and mantelpieces lightened with small coloured glazed tiles. Two-pin electric points show where standard lamps would have stood. In the kitchen an electric bell system replaced the wire-operated indicator of the previous generation. A small room opening onto the veranda completed the family rooms whilst the service rooms were placed to one side. Here, white glazed tiles, the labour-saving feature of the period, covered the wall behind the stove. The usual scullery and larder were nearby and a narrow coal store stood near the tradesmen's door at the side of the house. Upstairs were four bedrooms, each with a fireplace, and a small unheated room. A separate bathroom and lavatory were provided, the latter retaining its glazed white tiles finished with a black border.

This well-built brick house, rather formal in style – it included a small veranda with brick

and tile pillars supporting the roof in the manner of Lutyens – shows how local architects and builders adapted fashionable detail to the wishes and purses of their clients. For more modest suburban houses costs had to be kept within margins that were economically sound. Narrow plots of land meant lower costs and semi-detached houses further reduced the final price. In Recreation Ground Road, Newport, a pair of semi-detached houses and two single properties were built in the 1930s. The pair of houses shared a single gable roof, giving them the appearance of a wide-fronted house, with bay windows and Art Nouveau windows to lighten the stairs.

The detached houses were typical of architect designed houses of the time. The front door was set to one side under a tiled porch, opening into a spacious hall. The sitting room was in the front of the house, its size increased by the bay window which took up most of one wall. The parquet floor, glazed tiles around the grate, deep skirting board, picture rail and wide window sill completed a typical room of this date. Walls were treated in a much lighter manner than previously, often colour washed or covered with a plain textured paper, reserving decoration for borders and corners where flower patterns or modified Cubist designs brightened the plain surface. Wide-armed, deep-cushioned chairs and a settee made up the three-piece suite. Behind the sitting room, or lounge, the dining/living room had French windows opening into the garden, again representative of millions of suburban homes, but here the architect included a small veranda with a penthouse roof supported on wooden posts. The kitchen, a separate scullery for the deep, white sink and wooden draining board, and the walk-in larder, were set behind the hall with their entrance at the side of the house. Upstairs were the usual three bedrooms, a bathroom and lavatory. Stained glass windows in the hall and stairway provided one status symbol; the fine glazed cake stands and tea sets made by the short-lived Gunville Pottery during the 1920s and '30s offered another.

Such houses retained features of the vernacular movement, but the majority of local builders drew more on Edwardian 'old time' decoration in their efforts to provide an inexpensive house that was individual but not too different from its neighbours. Builders knew that most clients wanted a cottage-style house with modern conveniences. This was easy to achieve with pebbledash walls, tile hanging, add-on beams, and a whole range of porches – from those with penthouse roofs supported on posts, to the round brick arch and the immensely popular 'keyhole' porch. Windows also gave the house individuality.

A 1930s suburban house built in Newport is typical of architect designed houses built for the middle classes. The large bays lights the sitting room and stained glass in Art Nouveau style is used for the dormer window, shared by the bathroom and landing. The original garden fence can also be seen.

Many continued the Edwardian style, using coloured glass in the top lights of bay windows. The one modern feature local builders would consider were horizontal metal-framed Crittall windows, sometimes curved round corners as 'sun traps'. They were usually fitted under conventional roofs, but they do give added interest to a long run of cottage-type suburban houses, as can be seen in Old Road, East Cowes.

Suburban houses extended out of towns on main roads where mains drainage, gas, electricity and water services were easy to lay. The road from Newport to Cowes is a fragment of domestic history from this time. The houses were on a regular bus route but backed by green fields, giving easy access to work but in a rural environment. Sometimes Island suburbia was no more than a single road with semi-detached houses facing each other. Occasionally a miniature suburb appeared, perhaps only two or three roads, such as those near Newport's recreation ground, with tennis courts and cricket pitch, both essential parts of suburban life in the pre-war years.

Not all development was as modest as this. Sandown, Lake and Shanklin grew rapidly as convenient train and bus services attracted permanent residents. Ribbon development created one conurbation, comparable with suburban development on the mainland. New roads created a landscape of small houses and gardens, loved by the families who lived in them, loathed by the architectural establishment. But new houses such as those built in Sandown and Shanklin represented new hopes and aspirations for thousands of families, and local builders gave them the homes they wanted.

Even as the suburbs spread, the dream of a romantic village once more emerged. In July 1923 *The Isle of Wight County Press* included a notice that Alverstone Garden Village estate was to be planted on fifty-two acres near the Victorian village created by Lord Alverstone. Garden villages drew on the innovative factory villages of the nineteenth century and the planned Garden Cities of the twentieth century, such as Port Sunlight and Welwyn Garden City. At Alverstone, the new village required clearing much of Youngwood's Copse, part of the late Lord Alverstone's shooting ground. The promoters praised the situation, 'high above the village of Alverstone . . . magnificent views of the White Cliffs at Sandown . . . while behind the beautiful Brading downs.' More

practically, they assured prospective buyers that gas or electric light would be installed by means of a private plant. In addition, being on sandy loam, concrete blocks for building could be made from sand on the site, so dispensing with the cost of bricks. Plans for 107 bungalows were drawn up, as well as public gardens and a village hall.

At the opening of the village in October, Sir Edgar Chatfield Clarke, MP for the Isle of Wight, spoke of the shortage of houses and the need for smaller houses with 'labour saving devices' and adequately sized gardens. More significantly he mentioned the recent Housing Act which had introduced subsidies for smaller houses. Bungalows selling for less than £600 came within the terms of the Act, attracting a subsidy of £75 each. The bungalows at Alverstone fell within the regulations, meaning that the syndicate headed by Mr G. Frampton had some prospect of financial success when they began work. The official opening was completed when a date stone was set in the front wall of the first bungalow then being built, The Lodge.

The Lodge was built at the lower end of the copse, nearer to the old village, and slowly other bungalows advanced up the hill through the wood. Prospective buyers could choose their own plots and house design, but restrictions were enforced; no trade was allowed, no pigs could be kept and picket fences should be replaced by live hedges as soon as possible. The syndicate promoting the village wished the bungalows to be 'as artistic as possible', thus a thatched roof covered The Lodge's pebbledashed walls, and the front door was protected by a substantial porch supported on rustic posts. Although the bungalow looked small from the front it was surprisingly commodious. A sitting room and bedroom were separated by a passage which led from the front door to the kitchen at the back of the house. The kitchen had seven doors leading off

ABOVE The Lodge, the first house built in Alverstone Garden Village. The opening ceremony was held here in 1923 when a date stone was placed under the right hand window. This remains in place, as does the porch, although the house has been enlarged.

BELOW Woodside, Alverstone Garden Village, was one of the earliest bungalows built in the 1920s and remains almost unaltered. The roof was covered with asbestos tiles and one of the plank floors was found to have been laid over the bole of a tree!

it. Apart from the passage door and the back door there were doors to the larder, an airing cupboard, the bathroom, a back sitting room behind the front bedroom, and one which opened onto the stairs.

Not all the bungalows were as large as The Lodge. Woodside, on a corner at the top of Youngwoods Way, had an asbestos tile roof and a veranda to protect the front of the bungalow. The front door opened directly into the sitting room, whose brick fireplace provided warmth, whilst a vertical widow in the west wall gave extra light. Exposed black rafters gave a cottage atmosphere but the windows were modern metal casements. From here rooms opened into other parts of the house; one to the front bedroom, one to a back bedroom, a third to the bathroom and a fourth

This pretty bungalow in Mount Pleasant, Newport, includes the features buyers were looking for in the 1920s, gables with pebbledash and wood beams, a distinctive arch over the door and stained glass in the windows and in the door. This bungalow retains all these features, underlining the importance of windows and doors in maintaining the character of small houses which are part of our domestic history.

to the kitchen behind the sitting room. The pantry with the sink was off the kitchen at the back of the building, whilst under the roof of the back porch were the lavatory and coal house. It was a compact little home suitable for its occupants, two maiden ladies, both governesses, who gave private lessons to children, and perfectly represent the middle class families who moved to the Garden Village.

But this village was no more successful than earlier romantic housing schemes in the Island. By 1926 eight bungalows had been built, by 1935 there were only seventeen and no sign of the tennis courts and public gardens. The outbreak of war undoubtedly held back the development but more significant is the fact that only one of the early residents owned a car. There was one telephone owned by George Frampton, chairman of the syndicate, who allowed it to be used in emergencies. Although groceries, meat and milk were delivered the only public transport was by rail, and the station a good walk away. Isolation was the

inhibiting factor. Garden Villages were not rural villages, they were suburban and the people who were drawn to them did not want to live in an isolated copse miles from the nearest town. Alverstone had to wait until the arrival of the family car ended its isolation.

The choice of building, however, was significant. The bungalow was one of the most controversial domestic building styles of the twentieth century. 'Bungaloid growth' stretching outward into the green countryside was so alarming that in 1926 the Council for the Preservation of Rural England was founded to protect the rural landscape. But by this time such a cheap, easy to manage house was already established as part of our domestic architecture, and it has never been eliminated. The Indian colonial bungalow was the inspiration for the modern bungalow, although houses with only a ground floor had been built from the earliest years of the nineteenth century. Edwardian seaside bungalows led the way and after the First World War small cabins and shacks were set down in random fashion where space allowed. They scramble up the shore at Gurnard, piled up against each other as more and more filled the hillside. Nor were they restricted to the middle classes; a skilled workman at Samuel White's could afford to buy a plot of land at Thorness on which to build a small cabin for his family. It was the last of a long line of bungalows stretching out from Cowes towards Newtown – exactly what the CPRE so deplored.

Changes in society, especially the number of people living into retirement years with comfortable incomes, increased the demand for bungalows, as did smaller families. Government subsidies helped to keep prices reasonable and before 1939 three-bedroom bungalows could be bought for between £300 and £400, well within the price range of thousands of workers. The cheapest were flimsy buildings constructed with walls of

ABOVE Astolat, a new semi-bungalow at Whippingham, represents thousands of bungalows built between the wars. Half an acre of land was purchased with the aid of a mortgage from Newport Borough Council in 1937 and the house was built by S.W. Wendes, a Newport builder. Red brick walls and a red tiled roof were relieved by white paint and in the jointing over the door.

RIGHT Plan of the ground floor of Astolat, Whippingham. The compact nature of bungalows limited the arrangements of rooms. The lay-out was typical of bungalows in the 1930s.

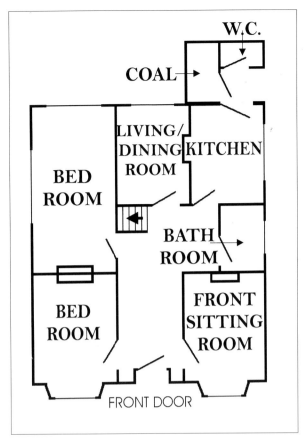

asbestos panels covered with roughcast and with asbestos tile roofs. Timber frame buildings clad with cedar shingle or a brick veneer, as well as conventional brick could be supplied to suit individual customers. The examples from Alverstone show how compact these houses could be and there was little scope for the builder to do more than arrange rooms within a basic shape. Clients still preferred a separate sitting room rather than one large living room, and the plumbing arrangements determined where the kitchen and bathroom should be.

The history of one well-built bungalow, Astolat, in East Cowes Road, Whippingham, might serve as typical of many bungalows in the Island. A mortgage was taken up in 1937 for half an acre of ground on which S.W. Wendes, a Newport builder, was to build the new home. A lime pit was opened on the site, bricks came from the Gunville works, red tiles covered the roof and under this a front sitting room, two bedrooms, a living/dining room, kitchen and bathroom were fitted into the ground floor. There was space upstairs for a third bedroom and a large loft area which might later be converted into a bedroom. Just outside the back door, but under cover, were the lavatory and coal house. The wishes of the prospective housewife were taken into account by the provision of Columbian pine for the interior wood fittings. She also chose the name for the new home, Astolat, the castle home of an Arthurian princess.

TWELVE

From Almshouses to Council Houses

The problem of how to house the lowest paid and poorest members of society has been a perennial one, and is not yet satisfactorily resolved. For most of our history the poor were conveniently seen as able-bodied, and obliged to fend for themselves, or deserving, that is the young, ill, disabled or old. For the latter the church, and later, secular society accepted responsibility. Almshouses represent the first subsidized housing. They were often associated with a church and built close by, but in other cases were administered by the town government.

This was the case in Newport, which had an almshouse by 1559. It stood on the north side of Sea Street, a narrow building with an eighteen-yard frontage but only nine feet deep. It was probably still in use in 1592, by when a second almshouse in a healthier part of town had opened. This was an old building at the junction of High Street and Pyle Street at the western limit of the town and by 1600 was Newport's only almshouse. It was occupied by 'poore widdowes' who had free accommodation and occasional gifts of money. A group of single-storey Victorian almshouses built in red brick with yellow brick banding and a central Gothic arch now stand very close to, or possibly on the site of the earlier almshouse.

In 1618 Giles Kent founded a second group of houses for five old people in Crocker Street. These were rebuilt in 1879 when Newport Corporation took over the charity. The style is typically Victorian picturesque, tiled roofs with decorative ridge tiles replaced the thatch, porches were added and diamond shape leaded window glass filled the casements.

Ryde's first almshouses were founded in 1856 by Mrs Augusta Wilder in memory of her husband. Sufficient money was provided to build three houses in Newport Street. Each could accommodate four women, widows or spinsters of good character, sixty years or older and native Islanders. The charity was originally attached to Newchurch parish and from 1868 to All Saints' church. These almshouses were finally demolished and replaced with modern flats, but the charity still helps in the work which continues there. In 1891 a further group of almshouses was founded in Ryde by Miss Harriet Player Brigstocke. These were three cottages built in Player Street to house six poor women, 'of good repute, blameless poverty but not paupers', a classic summary of the Victorian attitude to the poor. The charity was attached to Holy Trinity parish but, unlike others, was not rent free. The women paid 7p a week but were allowed, with permission, to take in lodgers. These plain and functional houses still exist, partly funded by the interest from Miss Brigstocke's original bequest.

The almshouses for elderly women in Cowes were founded in 1881 by the vicar of St Mary's, Thomas Macnamara. He built twelve almshouses for poor women in memory of his parents. His father had owned several plots of land in Cowes, including a small site off Market Hill where the houses were built. The

two-storey building with a formal garden in front was designed in the most picturesque style. The pretty original frontage remains, while the interiors are now modern flats. The original almshouses were single rooms with a scullery behind, but the ground floor tenants lost some privacy as the stairs to the upper rooms were placed on the inner walls of the

sculleries, perhaps explaining the rule stating that, 'Alms Women shall be kind and respectful to one another.' The tenants lived rent free and were granted a small pension. The pension was important, as they were not permitted to take in washing or ironing, the mainstay of many poor women.

The tradition of founding almshouses continued into the 1920s in the Island. Doctor Wyndham Cottle of Ningwood House, Shalfleet, died in 1919 and left a bequest to build almshouses on land he owned in Warlands Lane, Shalfleet. Two pairs of bungalows were designed by J.C. Millgate, a local architect, following the cottage style of the period. The buildings were brick with pebbledash and the front door into the living room was protected by a wood-framed porch. From this room, which was not large, one door led into the kitchen and another into two bedrooms. Compactness was contrived with amazing skill without detracting from the charm of these cottages, both inside and out. When the first tenants moved in they found rooms fitted with furniture bought at Wadham's, Newport, while linen, crockery and

A fisherman's cottage near Ventnor in the early years of the twentieth century. Time has ravaged what was a good stone house. Council houses were built to give families who lived in similar conditions good, sanitary homes.

utensils were also provided. Applicants were restricted to married Protestant men, over sixty, who had not received poor relief in the previous three years.

Almshouses could help only small numbers of the poor. Most old people remained at home and fended off poverty with small sums of poor relief and the help of friends and neighbours. The majority of poor people in the nineteenth century lived as their parents and grandparents had done; in tiny, dark and insanitary houses, whether these were rural cottages or in the narrow alleys and courts of towns.

It was only in the 1860s that the situation began to change in the Island. Country estates began to build improved cottages for their workers, following Prince Albert's lead at Osborne where a long-term programme of improving and building estate houses was instituted. These varied in style, from pattern book red brick Gothic for cottages on the main road into Whippingham, a more romantic row in Alverstone Road, and a fine pair using banded brick in New Barn Road, East Cowes.

The Nunwell estate built a row of picturesque cottages in East Ashey Lane in 1866, the initials HO on the date stone announcing that Sir Henry Oglander was the benefactor. The single block was built in stone, whilst an elaborate roof with five gables and dormer gables added to their attractiveness, showing the landowner as both generous and a man of taste.

In the west of the Island the Seely family was also building cottages. The family wealth was drawn from Nottingham coal, allowing Charles Seely to buy Brook House in 1856, together with a large estate in West Wight. The Seely cottages did not stand out in the landscape, but were built in a plain vernacular style in keeping with their surroundings. Stone with brick facings was used, with slate roofs, making them typical of their period. The staircase rose directly from the front door which had a room on each side on the ground floor and a scullery beside the kitchen. Two good-sized bedrooms were covered with a large attic space in the roof. Each cottage had a large garden, essential to a labourer's family. Charles Seely was a conscientious landowner, he kept the cottages in good repair and ensured that they all received free piped water.

A few miles away from Brook at Calbourne the Swainston estate was also building new houses in the 1860s. The memories of a fisherman's family who moved into one in 1862 allow us an insight into the improvement in living they brought to such people. Their old cottage at the mouth of Newtown river had no water supply at all. The new semi-detached cottage at London Heath had a shallow well and a further supply of fresh water about one hundred yards away. Their kitchen-living room had a built-in range and a separate pantry.

Attached to the house was a wash-house, shared by both families, with a brick fireplace and a pump for the well. Although the accommodation was much improved the family found fuel expensive, a never ending problem for the poor. They only bought coal in August when it was cheapest, and relied mainly on wood faggots from the Swainston estate, paying 42p for fifty bundles. The first tap was installed at the top of the garden in 1918 and was shared by four families: only in 1936 were a tap and shallow sink fitted in the pantry. Meanwhile, from the earliest days, the houses suffered from damp, the plaster flaked, the wallpaper came off, and only coconut matting survived on the floor. But Mrs Foss, the housewife, raised six children here, and every afternoon after work the scrubbed kitchen table was covered with a red cloth and the working room became a living room. This snapshot of one family could be repeated throughout the Island.

In the towns, housing for working people appeared on the fringes. The upper part of Ventnor (Lowtherville) began to be developed in the 1870s. Eighteen cottages of flint with brick facings were first built, the basic two up, two down house, with a front room and a back kitchen, two bedrooms overhead and outside a wash-house with a copper, and a lavatory draining into a cesspit. These houses were cheap to build and were rented at 25p a week in 1914 but, even so, many women had to take in washing to survive. Such houses held at bay the problem of housing the poor but even before the First World War it was clear that state intervention would one day be essential. From the early years of the century local medical officers of health began to report the true state of workers' housing.

In 1914 the Medical Officer for the Isle of Wight Rural District Council summarized the situation in the countryside. Overcrowding did not seriously affect the Island and could be overcome by encouraging cottagers to use the sitting room, 'which is seldom used, except for storing bicycles and perambulators', as a bedroom. The sitting room was to remain unused in many labourers' homes into the 1920s and 1930s, as they could only afford to furnish one living room. Sanitation was very bad, mostly a closet with a bucket. At Marks Corner, an isolated hamlet on the northern border of Parkhurst Forest, some mud-walled houses still remained, in such a poor state that they 'cannot remain as houses for human habitation for long.' Old 'picturesque thatched cottages' at Shorwell were also condemned, although the Medical Officer entered a plea that their repair, or any new building, should take account of the 'beauties of the place.'

The difficulty facing all housing reformers was the low wages paid to so many employees. It was this that defeated the first attempt to provide a modern worker's home in the Island. The plans came to the Island by a circuitous route. The founder of Bembridge School, J.H. Whitehouse, was closely involved in a scheme to design a model house for miners in his Parliamentary constituency of Lanarkshire during the 1914-18 war.

The architect chosen was Baillie Scott, who later designed the cottages at St Lawrence. He was asked to follow the principle that a worker's home 'should observe the same standards of health. . . as the greatest mansion'. In practice this meant light airy rooms, clean water, good sanitation and a bathroom. All these factors would later be essential elements of council housing, but when Whitehouse came to Bembridge in 1919 his belief that the cottage should serve as a model farm labourer's home failed, because the projected cost of about £250 was impossibly expensive. Instead, Culver Cottage at Bembridge School was built to the plan and two other cottages, Greenways at Hillway and Dolphin Cottage, St Helens, are modified versions of a design which divided the ground floor into two, with a living room in one half running from the front to the back of the house. The working space fitted into the second half of the house, including a bathroom entered from the scullery/kitchen. This was planned deliberately so that no dirt brought home by the husband was carried into the living room. Near the back door was the earth closet, entirely practical at a time when mains sewage was decades away in the countryside.

The 1924 Housing Act empowered local authorities to provide homes for rent and granted subsidies of £12.50 for each house built to an approved standard in rural areas. This was particularly important to the Isle of Wight. The rural district still had the highest number of dilapidated houses with low ceilings and small windows. Within a year six houses at Gunville were nearing completion and houses at Shalfleet and Freshwater were already built. The Council had no design staff and it worked with local architects and builders. This may explain why these early houses were not cheap. In 1927 the cost of proposed houses for Bembridge and Godshill were restricted to £450 each, £50 less than those at Gunville. The high cost of building brought problems in its wake, as rents had to reflect the outlay. When Carisbrooke parish requested six more houses at a rental of less than 42p a week the application was refused.

The cost of building fell in the 1930s. This brought recommendations from the Ministry of Health that tenders of no more than £250 for two-bedroom houses, and £300 for those with three bedrooms should be accepted. But the Rural District Council was prepared to take a robust stand against Ministry directives. In 1935 it refused to modify plans for six houses at Godshill costing £340. Their architect advised that modifications suggested by the Ministry would make the kitchen too small and the 'entrance into the bathroom very cramped'. The Ministry complained about 'parlour houses', those with sitting rooms, then being built at Chale at the same price. The clerk to the Council responded with the valid point that pairs of cottages built in small hamlets could not compare in cost with large urban projects. They could not be built at the recommended price, 'except of such inferior construction as the Council are not prepared to recognize.' Councillor Fred Hollis added that 'the Council was engaged in slum clearance, not building slums.' But the Ministry could also intervene for the benefit of the tenants. In 1936 plans for proposed houses for Freshwater, Winford, Newchurch and Calbourne had to be revised to increase bedroom space to meet overcrowding regulations.

Rents charged to tenants varied. Those in Heathfield Road, Freshwater, well constructed, larger than usual, with a hot water system and 'in a superior position' were rented at 55p a week. Houses at Godshill of a cheaper construction were 35p and council houses at Chale Green had exceptionally low rents of 17p as they were built under a Special Exchequer Grant for slum clearance. Internal maintenance for Rural District houses was shared between the Council and the tenants. In 1935 Brading tenants were supplied with new wallpaper to re-cover the sitting room and staircase walls. When Rookley houses were found to be dirty in 1937 the Council provided distemper and the tenants did the work. In the same year tenants at Bembridge suggested names for their houses instead of numbers and this was allowed.

But for many rural workers the rents remained beyond their means. In the early 1930s farm labourers in Bowcombe valley near Carisbrooke could earn £1.50 a week rising by 25p in 1937. In many cases labourers lived rent-free in 'tied' cottages owned by their employers, but their real need was for higher wages to spend on food and clothing. Large gardens provided families with potatoes and

Pre-war council houses built in Calbourne by the Rural District Council. In the 1930s government subsidies allowed local councils to begin a serious policy of rehousing families. These semi-detached houses in Elm Lane were built to government standards which ensured that there was no overcrowding. Although plainly built they followed middle-class standards. The original windows were wood framed sashes.

vegetables and there was often a pig in the sty, ensuring a basic meal of potatoes, cabbage and bacon.

Although the Rural District Council was initially responsible for most council housing the situation changed in 1933 when large portions of the rural district were transferred to borough and urban councils, giving them more land on which to build. But they, too, had begun to build houses in the late 1920s. In Newport the first tenants moved into Elm Grove Estate in 1926. This well-chosen site, below Mountjoy in Whitepit Lane, over-looked allotments and had wide views to Parkhurst Forest. There was space for a neat front garden behind chestnut fencing and a good back garden. The semi-detached houses were brick built, the upper storey pebble-dashed, with breeze block inner walls and party walls. A bay window distinguished the

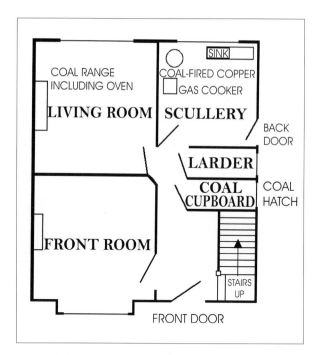

Ground floor plan of 67 Elm Grove Estate, Newport, a semi-detached council house built in 1926. It is now part of Whitepit Lane. The new council houses were well built with large windows, a scullery that was now virtually a separate kitchen and a living room from which cooking could be excluded. The coal hutch and coal cupboard meant that fuel was near to hand. This house had a bathroom and WC upstairs but in many council houses the bathroom was on the ground floor.

front room and a porch with a tiled roof protected the front door.

The interior followed a traditional plan with a narrow hall, stairs set on the outer wall and a front and back room. Family life centred on the living room behind the front room, with its Kuxswell coal range and a wide window opening into the garden. Beside the living room, at the back of the house, was the kitchen with is coal-fired boiler and gas cooker. A walk-in larder with a concrete cool shelf was off the hall, and on the outside wall next to the side door was the coal cupboard, which was filled from a hatch set at shoulder height. Two good-sized bedrooms each had tiny fireplaces, 'only used in dire emergencies', and the third

bedroom was unheated. There was an upstairs bathroom with a free standing bath on claw feet and a cold tap, a large gas geyser providing hot water. The bathroom also included a lavatory with a high cistern and a long chain. Houses of this type were at the top of council provision and were comparable with many privately built houses at this time.

One of the first tenants to move into the new houses was typical of those who could afford council houses, both in the Isle of Wight and throughout the kingdom. He was a postman who moved from an older house in Shanklin to Elm Grove. His work was secure and his neighbours, too, were the reliable tenants so attractive to local authorities; clerks, a carpenter and undertaker, an upholsterer and shop assistants in Newport stores. The rents were about 50p a week, to which had to be added the cost of gas which was paid with shillings put into a meter. It was these additional costs which families had not met before that put council houses beyond the reach of many. But the postman's family enjoyed on a modest scale the same advantages as middle class families. A weekly grocery order of 45p-50p was delivered, as was the meat, and bread came every day from a nearby bakery where a 3lb loaf cost just over 1p.

The Medical Officer of Health for Ryde summed up the difficulty relating to council housing in January 1928. 'It is impossible to eject people from a 5s a week slum and offer them one at 15s a week . . . the cheaper type are at present unavailable.' But already the Borough Council was making plans to build cheaper houses on land at Swanmore. In February approval came from the Ministry of Health to build ten pairs of houses on the north side of Bettesworth Road. They were typical of house plans adopted by many councils, with a living room, scullery, a bathroom with WC, a larder and coal house on the ground floor and three bedrooms. Gas was supplied to the

houses but no stoves were fitted. Although the cost of building each pair was approximately £800 the rents were deliberately kept low at 75p a week, excluding rates. The first tenants moved in during October. The Medical Officer of Health's report for that month records two families who were rehoused. Ivy Cottage, built behind two cottages in Daniel Street, Ryde, had two rooms and a 'dilapidated washhouse', and was the home of a young couple with children. In Quarry Road a two-up two-down house had been home to a family of seven. When the families moved to Bettesworth Road the old houses were demolished.

Behind this row of twenty houses the land was laid out in a manner that gave some justification to the mayor of Ryde's description of the development as 'The Garden City of Ryde'. The borough surveyor planned a square in which pairs of houses were set around a central island of houses, with the road curving round the inner space. It was a small gesture to suburban style and remains a distinct contribution to social housing. When the scheme was completed in 1929 sixty families had been rehoused, well above the target set by the Medical Officer in 1928.

In 1929 a small close of council houses was completed behind the more usual terrace of council houses in Bettesworth Road, Haylands, Ryde. The Ryde borough surveyor planned a square of semi-detached houses set around a small island of houses, an unusual scheme for council developments, drawing on Garden City ideas.

The 1933 Housing Act gave new impetus to local authorities to extend social housing. It was particularly directed to slum clearance, from which both Cowes and East Cowes suffered badly. In 1934 Cowes built 36 houses in Upper Mill Hill Road and at East Cowes the first council houses were built in Beatrice Avenue in the late 1930s. In all parts of the Island work continued to eradicate slum housing, but there was never a sufficient subsidy or money from rate revenue to make a concerted attack on poor housing. Most houses continued to be built privately for sale or rent, and although a start had been made in providing good housing for all it came to an abrupt halt in September 1939 when Britain declared war on Germany. It was to be many years before house building would begin again.

THIRTEEN

A New Start – Post-war Houses

A remarkable feature of the Second World War was the planning for post-war reconstruction which began in the earliest years of the conflict. In August 1941 Lady Denman, the national chairman of the Women's Institutes, wrote to her members telling them that plans for building were already in progress. This act of faith came to fruition in 1944 when the Dudley Committee on post-war housing issued its 'Housing Manual', a guide to good public housing, which was to influence local councils for many years. The need for new housing was there for all to see. In the Isle of Wight air-raids had destroyed or damaged over 11,000 buildings. Cowes and East Cowes suffered most with nearly 5,000 buildings attacked, but Newport, Sandown and Shanklin, and Ventnor each had over fifteen hundred buildings damaged or ruined. It was a daunting task that faced local councils.

Bomb damage in Shanklin. The effect of war damage meant that repairs to houses, and new building, were a priority in the immediate post-war period.

Such an immediate housing need brought an innovative response, the prefabricated house, small, cheap, with an imaginative use of interior space. In February 1945 two full-sized houses were set up in Ventnor Town Hall for housing committees to evaluate, but work on building these temporary homes was slow. Cowes and East Cowes overcame labour shortages by using German prisoners-of-war to construct the concrete bases. They arrived in September to work on sites in Mill Hill Road, Cowes and Victoria Grove, East Cowes. By July the following year thirty bases were ready at Victoria Grove and in August the Arcon Mark V 'temporary bungalows' arrived. They included cookers, washboilers and refrigerators, which replaced cool larders. Interior walls were to be painted banana colour, skirtings deep cream and ceilings cream. Outside doors and windows would be 'brilliant green'. But it was many more months before the first residents moved in.

Progress was slow everywhere. Ryde had been allotted fifty prefabs in November 1945. By October the following year only eight houses has been completed in Arundel Road, while in Great Preston Road slabs and hulls were all that could be seen. Shortage of labour defeated the best intentions and it was only in February 1947 that the prefabs in Victoria Grove were finally ready for occupation. These modern, stylish houses were much admired. They offered working people, for the first time, a really up-to-date home. In 1957 residents of Ryde had the opportunity to buy their prefabs at £150 each, with an anticipated future life of fifteen years, but these temporary houses continued to be lived in for many more years, and some may still be seen in use as farm buildings.

For years after the war ended shortage of labour remained a problem. The German prisoners at Cowes and East Cowes were repatriated in 1947 and local labour was hard

A pre-fabricated house at East Cowes in 1994, the final year of its life as a domestic dwelling. Introduced as a temporary measure in the late 1940s the pre-fab proved to be a highly successful small house, much admired for its modern kitchen lay-out and compact modernity.

to find. Nor was shortage of labour the only problem. Conventional house building was hit by a serious shortage of softwood in 1946, bringing orders from the Ministry of Health to replace timber joists and flooring with concrete. Lack of cement for rendering houses in Longmead Road, Ryde, held up work, hard plasterboard was unobtainable, roofing tiles in short supply and electrical fittings difficult to obtain. Problems went on into 1949 when supplies of bricks had to come from the London Brick Company at extra cost to Ryde Council. Savings were made by using breeze-blocks internally and cheaper facing bricks, but demand outstripped supply.

In the bleak years following the war food rationing was extended even to bread and the pressure to grow food made housing agricultural workers a priority. To encourage building the government granted a subsidy of £25 for agricultural houses, £9 more than that of council houses. Ryde housing committee was approached by a delegation from the Island branch of the National Farmers' Union in January 1947. Their secretary, Mr Sam

Watson, argued that new houses of a high standard were needed to encourage young people to stay on the land, but rents must be at an affordable level. Despite the importance of agricultural houses, it was the following year before consent was given to build five pairs of houses in Church Road, Havenstreet, at a cost of £2,575 a pair, and only in February 1949 were tenants able to move in.

A year later four pairs of agricultural workers' houses were built in Porchfield. Artificial stone was used for building but the vernacular tradition continued in the style of house and in the 100ft vegetable garden. The living-room/kitchen with a range and sink, and the 'front room', once the parlour, faced the front garden and were separated by the stairs. Behind them was the scullery, with a sink and copper, a larder, and a WC. Upstairs were three bedrooms and a bathroom with a handbasin and WC. The tenants were fortunate in having two lavatories, as recommended by the Dudley Committee; the following year economic decline saw the disappearance of a second lavatory in council houses. The plan of these houses has much in common with the eighteenth century cottage at Atherfield, and the tenant at number 3 lived in much the same way as his ancestors. He was a gardener on the Swainston estate, who as well as being the molecatcher did the coppicing in Elmsworth woods, improving his own garden with seaweed and leaf mould.

Immediately the war ended requests to improve council houses began. First were applications to replace kitcheners with open fires, always granted, as tenants paid for the work. During the 1950s deep, white sinks replaced shallow pre-war ones, and at the end of the decade electricity was taken to the bedrooms of older houses, or supplied to the whole building. Some families had to wait until 1960 before handbasins were fitted in their bathrooms, a luxury omitted in pre-war days.

Urban councils, however, had major projects in hand by this time. Large housing schemes were essential and preparatory work had begun in the Island before the war ended. In July 1944 Ryde housing committee was discussing possible sites for long-term housing. In November the Mayoress and three other women joined the committee to advise on the design and construction of the proposed new homes, a direct result of the Dudley Committee, which had been advised by women's organizations. In 1946 a site extending from Mayfield Road towards Binstead was chosen for major development.

In December 1948 C.A.F. Sheppard, a local architect, was appointed to design the layout and house plans. By June the following year the plans were approved, although Mr Sheppard had to amend the size of bedrooms to meet Ministry of Health standards, as pre-war architects had done. Tenders for the first sixteen houses came in by December 1950 but almost immediately severe economic conditions saw drastic reductions in costs. Out went the second WC, almost all cupboards, and the dresser in the kitchen and internal distempering. It was a depressing start but the first four houses were completed in Shepton Close by October 1951, when they were furnished by local firms and opened for the public to admire. Ryde had a long-standing sense of civic pride in its housing and this was shown again when a service of dedication was held to commend the future of this large housing development.

In the 1950s Newport began to develop land at Staplers, on a site overlooking the town. E.L. Smith, the architect of the vicarage at Lake, designed the early houses, continuing a traditional style. Twenty-eight houses were built in pairs and short terraces with a central passage to the back, while plans were prepared for blocks of flats and old people's bungalows, creating the mixed housing Government

A corner of Pan Estate, Newport, showing the lavish use of space council estates could provide in the 1950s. The early houses on this estate were designed by E.L. Smith, the Newport architect who designed Lake Vicarage. Middle class values were inevitably included in the new council houses.

required. At Newport brick was used for building but the Binstead houses included some in reproduction Island stone, which was widely used to solve the brick shortage.

Both these developments used space generously, with wide grass verges and green open spaces. The houses were well placed, those at Binstead facing the main road being carefully arranged with an exceptional area of grass before them. In Newport the Pan estate at Staplers continued a style of council housing which achieved a high standard in the 1930s. To walk through the roads and crescents today is to savour the last of a tradition which had its origins in the planned garden suburb.

The new estates included special categories of workers. Police houses were provided at Pan and flats for district nurses. In 1960 Columbia Products came to Binstead, requiring houses for their key workers, each house subsidised by £24. But the greatest problem in housing workers was at East Cowes. Here Saunders-Roe determined to end a chronic shortage of workers' houses by forming a separate company, the East Cowes Housing Association. Together with Cowes Urban District Council, the company planned to build 120 houses, the largest proportion of tenants to be company employees. The first 50 houses were completed by June 1950. They were Wimpy No Fines concrete houses, quick and easy to erect, but an emergency measure only. Building ceased until traditional materials were available. Three years later, Mr V. Aldridge, a Newport architect, prepared plans for an estate of traditional three-bedroom houses, and in 1954 work began using both brick and reproduction Island stone. The final number of

Chert, near Ventnor, built in the late 1960s adopted the spare lines of pre-war modern style. Ventnor architects, Gilbert and Hobson designed a horizontal building divided into two equal living areas for two retired ladies. Now holiday visitors to this National Trust property enjoy Miss Haddock and Miss McDowell's original home.

houses was reduced by ten to give sufficient green space in the development. Saunders-Roe is remembered in the naming of roads. Princess Close, where the concrete houses were built, commemorates the Princess flying boat and Broadsmith Avenue, where brick houses were built, honours Harold Edgar Broadsmith, a distinguished Technical Director.

Between 1945-1960 new housing was mainly the province of local authorities. When building licensing ended in 1954 private building was still restricted by shortages, but the future lay with owner-occupiers. In the mid-1980s 63% of homes, nationally, were owned, or being bought on mortgages. By this time, too, sale of council houses was general, a policy which had been encouraged since 1954. In September 1955 Ryde council sold nine houses at prices between £900 and £1,570, the forerunners of many later sales.

In 1939 the most striking addition to domestic architecture in the Island was Osborne Court, Cowes, and in the late 1960s this modernist style was chosen for a seaside home near Ventnor. It was still an unusual choice, but the austere design prepared by Ventnor architects, Gilbert and Hobson, proved to be starkly fitting in the lush Undercliff. 'Chert', now a National Trust

Fort Albert was completed in 1856 as part of the Victorian coastal defence of Portsmouth dockyard. In 1885 experimental work on the Brennan Locomotive Torpedo, the first true guided missile, was carried out here. Now the fort is domesticated and the owners of modern flats enjoy sea views to Hurst Castle.

property, was a horizontal building with living rooms set at first floor level. A spiral staircase with open aluminium treads and iron handrail was the centre of the house, which was divided into two mirror image parts. Miss Haddock and Miss McDowall, the two friends who lived here, each had a kitchen, bathroom and two living rooms. Bedrooms were omitted as bed-settees gave each lady a bed-sitting room. A wall of windows looked out to sea, pouring light into this late twentieth century version of the earlier marine villa.

The last quarter of the twentieth century saw the re-use of redundant buildings as new homes. Unlikely candidates were Palmerston's forts but two have found a new life; one at Spithead is a luxury home and Fort Albert to the west of Colwell Bay is now a complex of

flats with sea views. In Ventnor the long-closed cinema may provide yet more flats. Dramatic changes in agriculture made many old barns unusable and their conversion into domestic buildings was often controversial. But well conceived plans which respected the importance of entrances, air vents and building material made change to modern use a success. One of the earliest conversions was the barn at Shalfleet Manor, where Malcolm Pinhorn created a library and study in the mid-1960s, using large areas of glass to replace the old entrance. The best conversion of barns into homes followed this principle so that the character of the original has not been wholly lost. Where an ancient barn has been completely changed it would have been wiser to have adopted Robert Worsley's scheme at Appuldurcombe and leave 'not one stone standing', using them, as he did, to build a new house.

The appeal of the past has governed the last decades of the twentieth century. Old country cottages became treasure trove from the 1970s,

The seventeenth century barn at Shalfleet Manor, now a family home. This conversion has kept the character of the barn. The porch remains, the door filled with glass, air vents have been kept, and the new windows and roof lights are plain and simple.

when their selling prices spiralled upwards. More recently, town cottages have been 'gentrified', putting them beyond the reach of families whose recent ancestors would have lived in them. Some houses have been built in a complete historic style. A modern early nineteenth century villa in Ducie Avenue, Bembridge, and an eighteenth century farmhouse at Marvel, near Newport are examples. At Newclose Farm the owner-builder approached the project in a true eighteenth century manner, landscaping the ground, creating two small lakes and planting an avenue of trees from the entrance gate to the plain brick-built house, with its central door and regularly placed windows. In Castle Road, Cowes, eight terrace houses have been built with round-headed doors and first floor balconies with verandas and canopies, looking back to the great days of the yachting town.

A walk through any recent private residential development is to see a mixture of Victorian and Edwardian features added to the houses; terracotta ridge tiles, finials, dormer windows, black beams pinned to white plaster or brickwork. They are clearly intended to give houses that individuality which pre-war householders also wanted in their homes. This desire for individualism can be associated with a long-term trend, beginning in the post-war years when enforced higher standards in council housing closed the gap between private and public housing. Today Housing Associations replace councils in providing homes to rent and some of their building projects continue to be models of good housing. In Whitepit Lane, Newport, houses built in the old quarry continue the vernacular style of pre-war council houses, but they, too, are decorated with yellow brick banding borrowed from the Victorians.

Late twentieth century houses continued to look back to Edwardian and Victorian time as this house in East Cowes shows. Private housing demanded more individualism as the distance between their homes and public housing narrowed.

Grandparents who grew up in pre-war suburban houses, and parents who lived in houses built after 1961 will know that their children's houses have shrunk. New estate houses are smaller and closer to each other to keep prices within reach of prospective customers. But they are substantially better heated, so that bedrooms can now be used as all-purpose spaces throughout the year. And central heating has made one significant change to the external appearance of new houses; roofs without chimneys are becoming commonplace.

But it is within homes that the greatest change from the past is seen. The 'fitted' kitchen', a labour saving room, became a standard fixture from the 1970s. The utility room replaced the scullery, the refrigerator and

freezer replaced the larder and the *en-suite* bathroom replaced the dressing room. In many new homes the dining room has disappeared and meals are eaten in the kitchen, or before the television set in the living room. This reflects, perhaps, the greatest change in family use of the home, when both parents often work and children have diverse interests, so that many families no longer sit round a family table for the main meal of the day.

If we look for the most successful survivor in housing style in the past hundred years, the prize must go to the bungalow. The Council for the Preservation of Rural England were prescient in their alarm at pre-war 'bungaloid growth', but the battle was lost from the outset. The bungalow meets the same needs now as it did in the 1930s, but with much greater demand. Small families, single home-owners and many more pensioners all see them as ideal homes. They transform villages. Coach parties driving through picturesque villages such as Godshill and Brighstone are unaware

Langtry Place, Cowes. This is a twenty first century development where eighteenth century weatherboarding and early Victorian balconies show the enduring influence of the earliest days of seaside holidays in the Isle of Wight.

of the large estates that lie behind them. The bungalow managed to combine the idea of a rural cottage with a modern, warm, labour-saving interior. It has carried the idea of the cottage into the new century and seems likely to survive for many years to come.

In looking back over one thousand years of domestic building in the Isle of Wight we can see that four walls and a pitched roof have been, and remain, the expectation of most homeowners. Such a long history speaks of the practicality of such a building in a damp and temperate climate.

Much more, it reveals an unspoken sense of history which finds security in the past and expects domestic architecture to reflect this. It should not be impossible to continue the tradition, but there is clearly an opportunity now for imagination to combine this devotion to the past with a domestic style that is truly of the twenty-first century.

Further Reading

Arnold, Dana ed., *The Georgian Villa* (1998)

Barrett, Helena and Phillips, John, *Suburban Style, the British Home 1840-1960* (1987)

Basford, Vicky, *Historic Parks and Gardens of the Isle of Wight* (Newport 1989)

Boyton, L.O.J., *Appuldurcombe House English Heritage Handbook* (1986)

Brinton, Marion, *Farmhouses and Cottages of the Isle of Wight* (Newport 1987)

Brown, R.J., *English Farmhouses* (1982)

Burnett, John, *A Social History of Housing 1815-1985* (1980)

Cave, Lyndon F., *The Smaller English House* (1981)

Hockey, S.F., *Quarr Abbey and its Lands 1132-1631* (Leicester 1970)

Hockey, S.F., *Insula Vecta* (1982)

Lloyd, Nathaniel, *History of the English House* (1975)

Lyall, Sutherland, *Dream Cottages from Cottage orné, to Stockbroker Tudor* (1998)

Marshall, John and Wilcox, Ian, *The Victorian House* (1978)

Muthesius, Stefan, *The English Terrace House* (Yale 1982)

Rackham, Oliver, *The History of the Countryside* (1986)

Richards, J.M., *The Castles on the Ground, the anatomy of Suburbia* (1973)

Rubinstein, David, *Victorian Homes* (1987)

Searle, Adrian, *The Isle of Wight at War 1939-1945* (1989)

Sherfield, Ian, *East Cowes Castle the seat of John Nash Esq.* (1994)

Stone, Percy G., *Architectural Antiquities of the Isle of Wight* (1891)

Tomalin, David, J., *Roman Wight, a guide catalogue* (Newport 1987)

Whitehead, J.L., *The Undercliff of the Isle of Wight* (1911)

Woodforde, John, *The Truth about Cottages* (1979)

Romans on the Wight, (Isle of Wight County Council 1992)

JOURNALS

Cornforth, John, 'Balancing Past and Present, the country house between the wars', *Country Life*, 8 January 1987, pp 80-84

Hussey, Christopher, 'Mottistone Manor, Isle of Wight', *Country Life*, 16 March 1929, pp 362-368

Jones, Johanna, 'A survey of the Manors of Swainston and Brighstone, Isle of Wight, 1630', *Proceedings of the Isle of Wight Natural History and Archaeological Society 11 (pub. 1993),* pp 61-83

PRIMARY SOURCES

*Annual Report on the Health of the Rural Sanitary District of the Isle of Wight,
    1911*

Isle of Wight Rural District Council Minute Books, 1926-1928, 1935-1938, Isle
    of WightRecord Office

Ryde Council Minute Books, 1924-1929, I.W.R.O.

Ryde Sanitary and Public Health Committee Minutes, 1924-1927, I.W.R.O.

Ryde Housing Committee Books, 1944-1961, I.W.R.O.

Newport Council Minute Books, 1949-1960, I.W.R.O.

Housing Manual 1944, HMSO 1944

Acknowledgements

This book could not have been written without the generous help of many people over the years. The students who attended my courses on local history widened my knowledge of Isle of Wight houses, and the many householders who welcomed a complete stranger into their homes have all contributed to the wealth of information from which I have drawn in writing this short history of Island houses.

To them and to the following organizations and individuals I give my thanks; The Isle of Wight Council Museums Service, David Tomalin and Frank Basford; The Isle of Wight County Record Office and Richard Smout, the County Archivist; The Trustees of Carisbrooke Castle Museum, Rosemary Cooper, Curator and Glen True; The National Trust and Carol Pickett; East Cowes Heritage Centre and Sara Burdett; The Governors of Ryde School; Molly Attrill for her Open University study of Osborne Court; Mr and Mrs D Attrill; Keir Foss; Mr and Mrs D. Peel; Oliver Mathews; Laura Humphrys; the Revd. D. Menniss; Mr E. Toogood; Mr D. Barnes; Mr and Mrs D. Martin; Mrs Mona Norman; Mr R. Jolliffe; Mr and Mrs C.A. Tomlinson; Mrs L. LLewelyn; Mr and Mrs G. Dye; Mrs G. Postma; Mrs P. Brennan; Dr and Mrs Brooks; Mr and Mrs Willis; Mr and Mrs Leonard; L. and K. Ruthven; Mr and Mrs C. G. Longford; Mr W. Garnett; the Revd. R.M. Smith; Mr and Mrs J. Higgins; Mr and Mrs T.J Jackman; Mrs Thelma Ireson; Jack and Rita Plucknett; Mr D. Saxsby; The Vicar and Churchwardens, St Mary's, Cowes; Mr J. Edmunds; Margaret Rylands; Mrs Ella Simpson; Christopher Scott; Don French; Peter Atkinson.

Particular thanks must go to David Burnett, my publisher, for editing the text with the reader in mind, to my husband Jack Jones for preparing the Index, and to Roy Brinton who introduced me to many houses, gave me use of his library and his collection of prints and photographs of the Isle of Wight.

Index